and then shall the end come . . .

Table of Contents

Preface

I AM OFTEN ASKED whether we are living in the last days. It seems people everywhere have an unsettling sense that something is about to occur, but really don't know what it is. This question is most often accompanied by fear and concern. Invariably, when a serious news story unfolds in the Middle East, I get phone calls from people asking if the situation will escalate into the battle of Armageddon, and naturally, they are afraid. There was a time not long ago when serious news-making events were few and far between. We gathered around our television sets with great anxiety, watching and wondering what the world was coming to. Now hardly a day passes without something newsworthy happening somewhere in the world. However, today, in our desensitization, we shake our heads in despair and no longer question what the world is coming to, but how it can possibly go on.

What is happening? Why is there still no peace on earth? Why are false messiahs popping up everywhere? Why has our weather gone berserk? And why is El Niño blamed for every weather calamity on earth when most people had never heard of it prior to the nineties? We will discover the answers to these questions and many more as we turn to Scripture, the only reliable Truth. What is happening in our world today was foretold thousands of years ago, and despite assertions to the contrary, the Word of God really does provide a detailed road map of what lies just around the corner.

I am thrilled to tell you, as believers, we are the generation who will see the return of Christ. While we can expect the conditions on earth to steadily worsen, we have the blessed assurance of being spared the coming Tribulation. The world in all its chaos and wickedness would have us believe there is no God, or at least He is not in control. But our God is living and sovereign, and they simply fail to see what is happening in the world today is in prophetic fulfillment of His Word. I urge you to "stand fast, and hold the traditions which ye have been taught" (2 Thess. 2:15), "that, when he shall appear, we may have confidence, and not be ashamed before him at his coming" (1 John 2:28).

For those who have not trusted in Jesus as Lord and Savior, time is running out. The Bible tells us, "For the wages of sin is death; but the gift of God is eternal life through Jesus Christ our Lord" (Rom. 6:23). Nearly two thousand years ago, God came into the world in the form of a man, Jesus Christ, to pay the price for sin. In His infinite love for all of us, no matter who you are or what you have done, He willingly placed our sin on Himself and died so that we may live eternally. Because God is holy and we are born with a sin nature, we cannot come into His presence unless our sin is atoned for, and that is exactly what Jesus did on the cross. Placing our trust in Him as Lord and Savior enables us to get to God. Jesus assured us, "I am the way, the truth, and the life: no man cometh unto the Father, but by me" (John 14:6).

Salvation is freely given to everyone who acknowledges this truth and believes in their heart God raised Him from the dead. By placing your trust in Jesus, you are completely forgiven of every sin you have ever committed or will commit in the future. They are remembered no more, ever. We are promised, "As far as the east is from the west, so far hath he removed our transgressions from us" (Ps. 103:12), and "through his name whosoever believeth in him shall receive remission of sins" (Acts 10:43). But the time is drawing near when tremendous persecution and certain death will accompany salvation. I plead with you to delay no longer in asking

Jesus to come into your heart. In so doing, you too will be spared the coming Tribulation, and moreover, eternal separation from God.

With prophecy unfolding at an unprecedented rate and the "signs of the times" frequently occurring, I write these words of truth and hope for believers everywhere awaiting the return of Christ. Indeed, Jesus is coming to receive His Bride unto Himself, and we should have exciting tranquility in our hearts in the midst of all the worldly chaos we are experiencing. Scripture warns us of what is happening today and what we can expect of tomorrow.

It is my prayer that all who read this writing will lay aside any doubt or skepticism and open your hearts and minds to the truth of God's Word. His truth is not based on whether we believe; but rather, we believe because it is based on truth.

—Dr. John R. Bisagno

If any man have an ear, let him hear.

—Revelation 13:9

Knowing this first, that there shall come in the last days scoffers, walking after their own lusts, And saying, Where is the promise of his coming? for since the fathers fell asleep, all things continue as they were from the beginning of the creation.

—2 Peter 3:3–4

Introduction

ONE CAN HARDLY turn on a Christian radio or television broadcast without hearing someone talk about the end times in which we are living. Nearly three thousand years ago, the prophet Amos wrote, "Surely the Lord GOD will do nothing, but he revealeth his secret unto his servants the prophets" (Amos 3:7). God has impressed on the hearts of spiritual leaders everywhere an urgency to deliver the message that Jesus is coming, and come He must. The Second Coming of Christ is the central event toward which all of history is moving and without which none of history makes any sense.

Over the last thirty years, countless books, magazines, and newspaper articles have been written on prophecy. Unfortunately, those who foolishly set dates and times for the return of Christ have only served to cause confusion. As each of those dates came and went, excitement turned to skepticism to the point that today most nonbelievers, and even a host of believers, give little regard, oftentimes scoffing, when mention is made of Christ's imminent return. This very mockery is in fulfillment of the apostle Peter's prophetic words written over nineteen hundred years ago: "Knowing this first, that there shall come in the last days scoffers, walking after their own lusts, And saying, Where is the promise of his coming? for since the fathers fell asleep, all things continue as they were from the beginning of the creation" (2 Pet. 3:3–4).

Adding to the confusion are the well-intentioned, yet misguided individuals who have offered incorrect interpretations of Scripture, basing their positions on a single verse rather than applying the Scriptures as a whole. As a result, theories and speculations abound, and unless someone has a passion to perform the in-depth study required in order to fully understand what God's Word says about end-time prophecy, most are left to wonder who is actually right in their individual interpretations. Peter wrote, "some things hard to be understood, which they that are unlearned and unstable wrest" (2 Pet. 3:16).

I can only hope this book will clear up a lot of the confusion. Scores of resources are available to anyone who wishes to know the various viewpoints regarding end-time prophecy. I will not endeavor to expound on them since they are of no significance to the material contained in this writing.

I espouse a full pre-Tribulation Rapture viewpoint, a complete seven-year Tribulation period, followed by the one thousand-year millennial reign of Christ. To many, these terms may be unclear at this point, but as we progress, explanation will be given of their meaning and where they are supported in the Scriptures.

Indeed, God's Word reveals end-time prophecy with amazing attention to detail. My purpose in writing is to provide a clear understanding of these prophecies, placing them in their chronological order beginning with the signs of the times in which Jesus warned, followed by the Rapture of the Church, and including everything in between to the New Jerusalem, which will descend out of heaven to a newly created earth where believers will live for eternity.

When the Tribulation begins, prophecy will unfold rapidly. "For he will finish the work, and cut it short in righteousness" (Rom. 9:28). Many of these prophecies will occur simultaneously. As such, it will be noted when these events overlap. While current events substantiate that we are living in the last days and must therefore be included in any book on prophecy, this writing will not center around today's newsmakers, but rather, in light of today's unsettling events, what God's Word says is going to happen next.

All scripture is given by inspiration of God, and is profitable for doctrine, for reproof, for correction, for instruction in righteousness: That the man of God may be perfect, throughly furnished unto all good works.

—2 Timothy 3:16–17

Chapter 1

The Authenticity of the Bible

CAN WE REALLY trust what the Bible says, or is it full of errors and contradictions? A person's willingness to accept the truth of God's Word is related to their willingness to receive its Author. Usually those who attack the authenticity of the Bible are the very ones refusing to subject their lives to its authority. Most scoffers have never read the Bible, but instead have adopted the views of critics who discount it with ever-popular gems like, "It's something written by men, so it's full of errors," or "Everyone has a different interpretation of the Bible."

Someone once said, "Sin keeps a person from reading the Bible, and reading the Bible keeps a person from sin."

The fact of the matter is, the Bible convicts man's heart of sin, and rather than coming into agreement with God over our sinful ways and turning from them, many prefer the darkness over the light and deny the validity of the Bible so they may live as they please. We are assured, "How that they told you there should be mockers in the last time, who should walk after their own ungodly lusts. These be they who separate themselves, sensual, having not the Spirit" (Jude 18–19).

At no other time in its history has the Bible been under so much attack. Yet those who are driven with discrediting God's Word are simply in keeping with their very nature. The apostle Paul warned us that unbelievers "receiveth not the things of the Spirit of God: for they are foolishness unto him: neither can he know them, because they are spiritually discerned" (1 Cor. 2:14). He further added, "In whom the god of this world [Satan] hath blinded the minds of them which believe not, lest the light of the glorious gospel of Christ, who is the image of God, should shine unto them" (2 Cor. 4:4).

In fact, it is the work of the Holy Spirit who guides us into all truth (John 16:13), and when He comes to live in us, it is He who opens our minds to understand the Scriptures (Luke 24:45). In His high priestly prayer to the Father the night before He was crucified, Jesus included these words on behalf of all believers: "Sanctify them through thy truth: thy word is truth" (John 17:17).

Unbelievers cannot comprehend the Scriptures, and by denying the authenticity of the Bible, they consequently believe they are under no obligation to abide by its authority. In making the claims of interpretation issues or errors made by man in its translation, they necessarily influence the hearts and minds of others, who unwittingly adopt the same beliefs and spread these untruths without even bothering to open the Bible to see what it says for themselves. As a result, sin has become so prevalent in society that those who choose to obey God's Word and live under its authority are viewed as narrow-minded and intolerant, often the target of ridicule. Scripture is clear: "Whosoever transgresseth, and abideth not in the doctrine of Christ, hath not God" (2 John 9).

No other book has been banned, burned, or hated more than the Bible, yet it continues to outsell all other books. It is currently available, in whole or in part, in over eleven hundred languages and dialects. Many of these languages were reduced to writing solely in order that the Bible could be translated into their written format.[1] Over the centuries, countless men and women have died defending its truth, and Christians today have no less a responsibility in preserving its honor and authority as the Word of God.

Unfortunately, when believers are confronted with unfounded denial of the Bible's authenticity, many are ill–prepared to respond in its defense and usually feel defeated, wishing they knew what to say when the situation comes up again, or worse, avoiding the situation altogether. I encourage you to read *Why I Believe* by Pastor and author D. James Kennedy. His excellent book provides compelling and irrefutable evidence of the authenticity of God's Word, equipping the believer with a response to every objection he may hear.

The Bible was written by some forty different authors who were inspired by the Holy Spirit. It was written over a fifteen hundred-year period in the Hebrew, Aramaic, and Greek languages. These authors were spread over the continents of Asia, Africa, and Europe, with backgrounds ranging from fishermen to kings. Matthew was a tax collector. David was a shepherd. Paul was a rabbi and tent maker. Luke was a physician. Daniel was a prime minister. Peter, James, and John were fishermen. Amos was a farmer. Solomon was a king. Jeremiah, Ezekiel, and Zechariah were all priests. Most of these authors never even met each other, yet they all consistently wrote of a common theme, the redemption of mankind through the Lord Jesus Christ.

When we consider the possibility of this occurring, we are left to conclude there is no way this could be done unless it were written by God. If I were to select ten people from all walks of life and ask them to write a story on a common theme, without telling them the theme, of course I would receive ten papers with ten different themes. Even if I told the same ten people a story with its theme and then asked them to write a paper on it, there is no doubt I would receive ten different versions of how they perceived the story.

Despite the astounding facts of the Bible's consistent theme as recorded by forty different authors, there will nonetheless be skeptics who claim these authors read one another's writings, copying each other's works. But this view is wholly without basis and ignores indisputable evidence to the contrary.

People have also been brainwashed into believing science has disproven the Bible. In fact, science confirms the validity of Scripture. Sir Cecil Wakeley, one of the world's leading scientists, has said, "Scripture is quite definite that God created the world, and I for one believe that to be a fact, not fiction."[2] Millions of people the world over passionately cling to the theory of evolution without even realizing that many of those who originally espoused it ultimately abandoned their beliefs. In fact, Charles Darwin himself said, "The distinctions of specific forms and their not being blended together by innumerable transitional links is a very obvious difficulty."[3]

T. H. Morgan, an outspoken evolutionist, is quoted as saying, "Within the period of human history we do not know of a single instance of the transformation of one species into another. . . . It may be claimed that the theory of descent is lacking, therefore, in the most essential feature that it needs to place the theory on a scientific basis. This must be admitted."[4]

As well, Sir Julian Huxley, one of the world's leading evolutionists and a descendant of Thomas Huxley, an ardent colleague and follower of Charles Darwin, stated, "I suppose the reason we leaped at *The Origin of Species* was because the idea of God interfered with our sexual mores."[5]

Again, British evolutionist Sir Arthur Keith has said, "Evolution is unproved and unprovable. We believe it because the only alternative is special creation, which is unthinkable."[6]

Finally, physicist H. J. Lipson once stated, "I think however that we must go further than this and admit that the only acceptable explanation is Creation. I know that this is anathema to physicists, as indeed it is to me, but we must not reject a theory that we do not like if the experimental evidence supports it."[7]

I am always left to wonder why people are so willing to believe what so-called individuals of higher learning tell us when God's Word tells us otherwise. The apostle Paul wrote, "the wisdom of this world is foolishness with God" (1 Cor. 3:19), and, "The Lord knoweth the thoughts of the wise, that they are vain" (1 Cor. 3:20). Of course, we accept the world's words as truth because as laymen, we have no way of confirming what we are told.

For years, scientists told us the planet Saturn had seven rings. Of course we believed it. Why wouldn't we? They had the telescopes to confirm it. But it was not until the recent development of further space technology, enabling us to get a closer look at distant planets, that scientists were able to determine that Saturn, in fact, has a myriad of rings. Indeed, an in-depth study of the planetary system alone will convince the hardest skeptic of the existence of God. David wrote, "The heavens declare the glory of God; and the firmament sheweth his handywork" (Ps. 19:1).

So while we may depend on scientists to enlighten us in scientific matters, when it comes to spiritual matters, we must realize that many of these learned individuals are unbelievers and their opinions are tempered with the human perspective. Without question, where science and Scripture appear to conflict, we must always defer to God's Word as truth over the reasonings of man, for "it is better to trust in the Lord than to put confidence in man" (Ps. 118:8). The apostle Paul wrote, "your faith should not stand in the wisdom of men" (1 Cor. 2:5).

Finally, the Bible has been undeniably authenticated through archaeological finds. There have been over twenty-five thousand archaeological discoveries pertaining to the Bible, as well as tens of thousands of confirmed records regarding individuals and events recorded in the Bible.[8] Jewish archaeologist Nelson Glueck has said, "It may be stated categorically that no archaeological discovery has ever controverted a biblical reference."[9]

In 1977, Major General Chaim Herzog, former Israeli ambassador to the United Nations, was quoted as saying:

> Everywhere you turn in Israel today the Bible is coming to life. I'm not talking only about archaeological discoveries, but about the international political scene as it affects us today. If you read the biblical prophecies about Armageddon and the end days, and you look at the current realities in the world and especially in the Middle East, things certainly begin to look familiar. The vast number of archaeological discoveries in Israel have all tended to vindicate the pictures that are presented in the Bible. If therefore the Bible has been proven true concerning the past, we cannot look lightly at any prognostication it makes about the future.[10]

So can we trust what the Bible tells us? Indeed we can. Is it full of errors and contradictions? No way.

All scripture is given by inspiration of God, and is profitable for doctrine, for reproof, for correction, for instruction in righteousness: That the man of God may be perfect, throughly furnished unto all good works.
—2 Timothy 3:16–17

Endnotes

1. Steven Barabas, Th.D. (Princeton Theological Seminary), Professor of Theology, Wheaton College, Author: *So Great Salvation.*
2. Quoted in D. James Kennedy, *Why I Believe* (Word Publishing, 1980), p. 52.
3. *Creation-Evolution Encyclopedia*, "Origin of the Species Unknown," Creation Science Facts.
4. Quoted in D. James Kennedy, *Why I Believe*, p. 59.
5. Ibid., p. 52.
6. Ibid., p. 51.
7. *Creation-Evolution Encyclopedia*, "Origin of the Species Unknown."
8. D. James Kennedy, *Why I Believe*, p. 35
9. Ibid., p. 36.
10. Hal Lindsey, *The 1980s: Countdown to Armageddon* (Bantam Books, New York, 1980), p. 35.

Knowing this first, that no prophecy of the scripture is of any private interpretation. For the prophecy came not in old time by the will of man: but holy men of God spake as they were moved by the Holy Ghost.

—2 Peter 1:20–21

Chapter 2

Prophecy in the Bible

WE LIVE IN AN AGE of psychics and soothsayers, telling hopeful listeners what they want to hear regarding their future. God's Word is very clear about those who profess this ability, as well as those seeking direction from them. Moses warned the children of God, "There shall not be found among you any one that maketh his son or his daughter to pass through the fire, or that useth divination, or an observer of times, or an enchanter, or a witch, Or a charmer, or a consulter with familiar spirits, or a wizard, or a necromancer. For all that do these things are an abomination unto the LORD: and because of these abominations the LORD thy God doth drive them out from before thee" (Deut. 18:10–12).

Even though this instruction was given to the Israelites thousands of years ago, it still applies to believers today because the Bible tells us God is the same yesterday, today, and forever (Heb. 13:8), and that He changes not (Mal. 3:6). Though society changes, God remains the same, and we are never left to wonder where He stands on any given issue when it is written in His Word.

Christians are forbidden to seek clairvoyant guidance. It is not for us to know what will happen in our individual future. We are to depend solely on the provision of God and only seek answers to our questions through prayer and abiding in His Word for the direction we need in our everyday lives. All God wants us to know about the future is how it pertains to mankind as a whole, and just as all biblical prophecy up to now has been fulfilled with one hundred percent accuracy, so will be that which remains.

So what about all these psychics who possess the intriguing ability to see into the future, such as Nostradamus, Edgar Cayce, or Jeane Dixon? Doctors and scientists tell us we only use ten percent of our brain capacity, so perhaps the answer lies in their greater command of brain function. That may be, but I am more inclined to believe what the apostle Paul wrote. "Now the Spirit speaketh expressly, that in the latter times some shall depart from the faith, giving heed to seducing spirits, and doctrines of devils" (1 Tim. 4:1). In her book *The Beautiful Side of Evil*, Johanna Michaelsen reveals her own fourteen–month experience as an assistant to a psychic surgeon and how God showed her that the incredible healings she witnessed were directly attributed to evil shrouded in holiness.[1]

God's Word gives us the standard by which a prophet must be measured. Moses warned us how we could know for sure if those telling the future are from God. "When a prophet speaketh in the name of the LORD, if the thing follow not, nor come to pass, that is the thing which the LORD hath not spoken" (Deut. 18:22). In fact, if the prophecy does not come true, God's Word assures us, "the prophet hath spoken it presumptuously" (Deut. 18:22), meaning "overstepping due bounds" or "taking liberties," as Webster defines it.

And what of the channelers who claim to be talking to the departed? There certainly exists the spirit realm where Satan, the god of this world, rules. When a person foolishly elects to communicate with the spirits through the use of Ouija boards or seances, they are dealing with evil darkness, and are as such vulnerable to demonic forces of deception. The apostle Paul assures the believer, "to be absent from the body, and to be present with the Lord" (2 Cor. 5:8), not roaming around in some spiritual state waiting for someone to do something on our behalf so we may be released to our eternal abodes. And further, when anyone dies, their souls do not return to take up residence in another person's body. Scripture clearly states that "it is appointed unto men once to die, but after this the judgment" (Heb. 9:27). In the case of Lazarus (John 11:1–46), the widow of Nain's son (Luke 7:11–17), the synagogue official's daughter (Matt. 9:18–25), the disciple of Tabitha (Acts 9:36–41), Eutychus, who fell from a third-floor window (Acts 20:9–10), and all the saints who came forth from their graves at Christ's resurrection (Matt. 27:52–53), in every single case, the miracle of bringing them back to life was permitted by God as a witness of His power and to bring glory unto Himself. So there is a dark mystery to all the psychic phenomena, but it bears no relation to the light and goodness of God. Indeed, "God is light, and in him is no darkness at all" (1 John 1:5).

It is interesting to note those who claim to have the uncanny ability to see into the future never state dates and times or scores of ball games or anything near a specific prediction. Instead, they make broad predictions based on the odds of an event taking place. A psychic may state a plane will crash within the year, but they will not give the airline, the date, or any other specific information so we can all stay off that plane. I am certainly not clairvoyant, but with the congestion in airline traffic, our aging planes, the certainty of human error, and a number of other factors, even I can predict a plane will go down in the near future. Consequently, when the tragedy does occur, the psychic is touted as capable of telling the future, and proceeds to make a handsome living off of confused and desperate people in search of answers.

The Committee for the Scientific Investigation of Claims of the Paranormal (CSICOP), a nonprofit scientific and educational organization formed eighteen years ago, objectively examines claims of psychic or paranormal activity and publishes the results of their findings in a magazine entitled *Skeptical Inquirer*. Eugene Emery of CSICOP compiled a list of predictions from the top psychics of tabloid magazines such as *National Enquirer, Sun, Globe,* and *National Examiner.* Here are just a few predictions they had for 1996.

- While giving testimony in the civil suit, O. J. Simpson will confess to killing Nicole Brown Simpson and Ronald Goldman, and then become a minister.
- Middle East terrorists will kidnap Barbara Walters and free her after ABC gives them a three-hour platform to express their views, hosted by Barbara, of course.
- Michael Jackson will have a sex-change operation, insisting everyone refer to him as Michelle, while wife, Lisa Marie, stands by her man.
- Susan Lucci will win an Emmy but break a toe after dropping it on her foot.[2]

While these predictions are certainly amusing, not one of them came true. In fact, the accuracy rating of all psychics falls miserably short of perfection. Nationally renowned psychic Sylvia Browne, who has made the rounds on the talk-show circuit, chooses her words a little more carefully, but also missed the mark of perfection in her predictions for 1997. Here are just a few.

- A commercial airline leaving Egypt could be at risk of a bomb in April.
- Tornadoes in great number will devastate parts of Oklahoma, Kansas, and Missouri in April.
- Barbra Streisand will marry an actor. (She married actor James Brolin in 1998.)
- Hillary Rodham Clinton will be exposed in a scandalous longtime affair.[3]

Despite her inaccuracies, Ms. Browne has felt confident enough to map out mankind's future for the next one hundred years. Among her forty predictions, she foresees the following:

- Houses will be constructed with a third floor and a rollback roof to allow Hovercrafts the ability to come and go.
- Atlantis will slowly resurface around 2023 and become fully visible by 2026.
- The West Coast will *finally* fall into the ocean in 2026.
- Aliens will show themselves in the year 2010, not to harm us, but to see what we are doing to the earth and then reacquaint us with the antigravity devices we used to construct the pyramids.
- Peace will come in the year 2050 and last for fifty years until 2100 (when she fails to see anything beyond, attributing that to "the end will come like a thief in the night").
- No world war, no nuclear holocaust, just little skirmishes.[4]

In 1552, French physician and highly acclaimed psychic Michael Nostradamus predicted the end of the world would come in 3747. That would be 1,647 years later than Ms.

Browne's prediction, and that presents a problem. So whom shall we believe? Neither.

As we shall see, God's Word predicts a far different future for mankind, providing graphic and specific detail. And incidentally, He tells us there will be *no* real peace until Jesus returns to the earth, and, yes, all the nations of the world *will* come together in a final nuclear holocaust.

The Bible is God-breathed, His spoken Word to mankind. Over thirty-eight hundred times, the Bible says, "thus saith the Lord," "the Word of God," or "the Word of the Lord." Jesus said, "the Spirit of truth . . . will guide you into all truth: for he shall not speak of himself; but whatsoever he shall hear, that shall he speak: and he will shew you things to come" (John 16:13). That is why thousands of prophecies have been fulfilled with complete accuracy. This fact alone points to the undeniable truth and sovereignty of God. Outside of the prophetic Scriptures, without fail, no one has predicted the future with accuracy. Only God is able to do so, and tells us that in His Word. "Remember the former things of old: for I am God, and there is none else; I am God, and there is none like me, Declaring the end from the beginning, and from ancient times the things that are not yet done . . . yea, I have spoken it, I will also bring it to pass; I have purposed it, I will also do it" (Isa. 46:9–11).

Nearly one-third of the Bible relates to prophecy. In the Old Testament alone, over two thousand prophecies have already been fulfilled,[5] of which more than three hundred pertain to the birth, life, ministry, death, and resurrection of Jesus. Nearly a thousand years before its fulfillment, David relates his own struggle with death to what Jesus would eventually suffer. "For dogs have compassed me: the assembly of the wicked have inclosed me: they pierced my hands and my feet. . . . They part my garments among them, and cast lots upon my vesture" (Ps. 22:16,18). Incredibly, David is describing death by crucifixion, a Roman method of execution not to be introduced for another seven hundred years.

Of course, I encourage you to read the Scriptures daily and discover for yourself the rich treasure of God's Word. As you learn of prophecy and its fulfillment, you will be blessed with a renewed sense of trust in the faithfulness of God to do just as He promises.

The prophets in the Bible are referred to as major and minor prophets. The minor prophets are certainly of equal stature to the major prophets, only their writings are not as long. In the Old Testament, the Hebrew words *navi', ro'eh,* and *hozeh* all refer to a "spokesman of God." Their function as prophets is clearly stated. God says, "I will raise them up a Prophet . . . and will put my words in his mouth; and he shall speak unto them all that I shall command him" (Deut. 18:18). Here are just a few Old Testament prophecies from Isaiah, a major prophet, and Zechariah, a minor prophet, and where their fulfillment is found in the New Testament. Incidentally, *all* of the Bible's prophets had something to say about the world we live in today.

Referred to as "the evangelical prophet," Isaiah spoke continually of the redemptive work of Christ some seven hundred years before His incarnation. Interestingly, the name Isaiah means "salvation of Jehovah." Starting in 740 B.C., Isaiah's public ministry spanned a period of sixty years until his death at one hundred twenty years of age. He recorded many prophecies regarding the life of Christ.

> Therefore the Lord himself shall give you a sign; Behold, a virgin shall conceive, and bear a son, and shall call his name Immanuel.
>
> —Isaiah 7:14

Now the birth of Jesus Christ was on this wise: When as his mother Mary was espoused to Joseph, before they came

together, she was found with child of the Holy Ghost. . . .
And she shall bring forth a son, and thou shalt call his name
JESUS: for he shall save his people from their sins. Now all
this was done, that it might be fulfilled which was spoken
of the Lord by the prophet, saying, Behold, a virgin shall
be with child, and shall bring forth a son, and they shall
call his name Emmanuel, which being interpreted is, God
with us.

—Matthew 1:18–23

Surely he hath borne our griefs, and carried our sorrows:
yet we did esteem him stricken, smitten of God, and afflicted. But he was wounded for our transgressions, he was
bruised for our iniquities: the chastisement of our peace
was upon him; and with his stripes we are healed.

—Isaiah 53:4–5

. . . they brought unto him many that were possessed with
devils: and he cast out the spirits with his word, and healed
all that were sick.

—Matthew 8:16

But one of the soldiers with a spear pierced his side. . . .

—John 19:34

Then Pilate therefore took Jesus, and scourged him.

—John 19:1

He was oppressed, and he was afflicted, yet he opened not
his mouth: he is brought as a lamb to the slaughter, and as
a sheep before her shearers is dumb, so he openeth not his
mouth.

—Isaiah 53:7

And when he was accused of the chief priests and elders, he answered nothing. Then said Pilate unto him, Hearest thou not how many things they witness against thee? And he answered him to never a word; insomuch that the governor marvelled greatly.

—Matthew 27:12–14

I gave my back to the smiters, and my cheeks to them that plucked off the hair: I hid not my face from shame and spitting.

—Isaiah 50:6

Then did they spit in his face, and buffeted him; and others smote him with the palms of their hands.

—Matthew 26:67

The voice of him that crieth in the wilderness, Prepare ye the way of the LORD, make straight in the desert a highway for our God.

—Isaiah 40:3

In those days came John the Baptist, preaching in the wilderness of Judaea, And saying, Repent ye: for the kingdom of heaven is at hand.

—Matthew 3:1–2

Zechariah was a priest and an exile in the Babylonian captivity. He was called to be a prophet in 520 B.C. Zechariah means "the Lord remembers." Accordingly, the theme of his writing regarded the coming of the Messiah and the restoration of Israel.

And I said unto them, If ye think good, give me my price; and if not, forbear. So they weighed for my price thirty pieces of silver. And the LORD said unto me, Cast it unto the potter: a goodly price that I was prised at of them. And I took the thirty pieces of silver, and cast them to the potter in the house of the LORD.

—Zechariah 11:12–13

Then one of the twelve, called Judas Iscariot, went unto the chief priests, And said unto them, What will ye give me, and I will deliver him unto you? And they covenanted with him for thirty pieces of silver.

—Matthew 26:14–15

And he cast down the pieces of silver in the temple, and departed, and went and hanged himself. . . . And they took counsel, and bought with them the potter's field, to bury strangers in.

—Matthew 27:5,7

. . . Behold, thy King cometh unto thee: he is just, and having salvation; lowly, and riding upon an ass, and upon a colt the foal of an ass.

—Zechariah 9:9

. . . Go ye into the village over against you; in the which at your entering ye shall find a colt tied, whereon yet never man sat: loose him, and bring him hither. . . . And they brought him to Jesus: and they cast their garments upon the colt, and they set Jesus thereon.

—Luke 19:30,35

. . . Smite the shepherd, and the sheep shall be scattered. . . .

—Zechariah 13:7

. . . . Are ye come out as against a thief with swords and

staves for to take me? . . . Then all the disciples forsook him, and fled.

—Matthew 26:55–56

Of course, one may shrug his shoulders and suggest the fulfillment of these prophecies is mere coincidence, but the statistical probability of just these eight prophecies alone being fulfilled is one in ten to the seventeenth power, that is, one in 100,000,000,000,000,000 chances. When we consider that more than two thousand others have already been fulfilled, the odds become incalculable. The odds of these eight prophecies being fulfilled in the life of one Man are equivalent to filling the entire state of Texas knee-deep with quarters, then someone flying overhead in a plane dropping a dime into the pile, the quarters then being mixed and shuffled for two years, and a blindfolded man finding the dime on his first try.

The fulfillment of thousands of prophecies alone provides more than convincing proof that we can believe the Bible and trust its Author. At this pivotal time in history, there remain no other prophecies to be fulfilled except those pertaining to the end times, and they will be fulfilled as well. Jesus said, "For verily I say unto you, Till heaven and earth pass, one jot or one tittle shall in no wise pass from the law, till all be fulfilled" (Matt. 5:18). History is a record of events after they happen. Anyone can write history. Prophecy is a record of events before they happen, and none but God can write prophecy.

> *. . . I will hasten my word to perform it.*
>
> **—Jeremiah 1:12**

Endnotes

1. Johanna Michaelsen, *The Beautiful Side of Evil* (Harvest House Publishers, Eugene, Oregon, 1982).

2. Eugene Emery, CSICOP Press Release, December 1996.
3. Sylvia Browne, "1996 Predictions by Sylvia Browne," October 19, 1996, Sylvia Browne Corporation.
4. Sylvia Browne, "Predictions for the Next Hundred Years," April 1997, Sylvia Browne Corporation.
5. D. James Kennedy, *Why I Believe* (Word Publishing, 1980), p. 26.

. . . ye can discern the face of the sky; but can ye not discern the signs of the times?

—Matthew 16:3

Chapter 3

Signs of the Times

AFTER CHASTISING THE SCRIBES and Pharisees for their hypocrisy, Jesus left the Temple and began walking toward the Mount of Olives just east of Jerusalem. The disciples followed along, and while crossing the Kidron Valley, hoped to lighten the mood of things by pointing out to Jesus the beauty of all the Temple buildings. He responded with prophecy, telling them all the buildings would be totally destroyed, "There shall not be left here one stone upon another" (Matt. 24:2). When He reached His destination on the Mount, He sat down and the disciples gathered around. They began asking a series of questions regarding what He had told them along the way. They said, "Tell us, when shall these things be? and what shall be the sign of thy coming, and of the end of the world?" (Matt. 24:3).

Jesus revealed the answers to two of their questions in His apocalyptic sermon known today as the Olivet Discourse. The one question Jesus did not answer was when the Temple would be destroyed. Instead, His prophetic words were fulfilled approximately forty years later in A.D. 70 when the Roman general Titus conquered Jerusalem and completely destroyed it.

In the Olivet Discourse, Jesus revealed a number of signs to determine "the end of the world." Of course, any of the signs can be identified throughout history as isolated events here and there, but the *simultaneous* occurrence of the signs, combined with their frequency and intensity, depicts the benchmark to precede Christ's return. Jesus related the signs to birth pains (Matt. 24:8). When a woman is about to give birth, she experiences painful contractions which increase in frequency and intensity the closer she is to delivering her child. Just so, the closer we get to the return of Christ, the more frequent and intense the signs will become.

After announcing the "signs of the times" which precede His return, Jesus gave the parable of the fig tree. The fig tree is symbolic of Israel. He said, "When his branch is yet tender, and putteth forth leaves, ye know that summer is nigh: So likewise ye, when ye shall see all these things, know that it is near, even at the doors" (Matt. 24:32–33). He added, "Verily I say unto you, This generation shall not pass, till all these things be fulfilled" (Matt. 24:34).

Since the day Jesus ascended to the Father, Christians have been watching the skies for His return. Over the centuries, strange or unusual occurrences often triggered apocalyptic fervor, causing the uninformed to run around like Chicken Little, saying, "The end is near! The end is near!" Because of it, we are experiencing a "little-boy-who-cried-wolf" syndrome where few are listening anymore, when it really is the truth. And now that the new millennium has caught the attention of Hollywood, the seriousness of these end times has been relegated to mere sensational entertainment to scare its audiences, while seldom bearing any resemblance to the truth. The media has also done its share of diffusing all the end-time clamor by relating it to the same hoopla surrounding the turn of the millennium.

Though all the doomsdayers of old meant well, the fact is, the countdown to the end times could not even begin until a single event took place: the statehood of Israel. As the fig tree, Israel "became tender" on May 14, 1948. On that date, after some nineteen hundred years without a homeland, the Jews reunited to form the nation of Israel. This was a miracle of untold proportion. At no other time in history has a country ceased to completely exist and then later revive to form a nation. Mark Twain once said, "All things are mortal but the Jew; all other forces pass, but he remains. What is the secret of his immortality?"[1] The Jews continue to exist because God has a plan for them, and it centers around a covenant He made with Abraham over four thousand years ago.

During His Olivet Discourse, Jesus likened the attitude of the generation who would witness His return to the apathy of Noah's days when Noah warned the people of the impending flood, but "knew not until the flood came, and took them all away" (Matt. 24:39). Despite one hundred twenty years of warning beforehand, the people ignored Noah, laughing and ridiculing him as he constructed the ark and gathered the animals in by twos. After all, it had never rained on the earth up to that point, so obviously he must have been a lunatic. When the time came for Noah and his family to enter the ark, God closed the door behind them, and all the laughing and ridicule came to an end (see Gen. 6–7).

Just so today, despite all the words of warning, our apathetic generation simply will not take heed. Scripture speaks to this: "Behold, ye despisers, and wonder, and perish: for I work a work in your days, a work which ye shall in no wise believe, though a man declare it unto you" (Acts 13:41). Like

Noah, believers who proclaim Jesus is coming are oftentimes viewed as weirdos or lunatics, and we are left to carry the burden of the nonbelievers' fate, just as Noah and his family anguished over everyone outside the ark. As the unfamiliar rains descended and the waters rose, they likely pounded on the ark, begging to get in, all the while facing the sickening realization that his warnings had actually come true. And so it will be for all who have heard and chosen to ignore the warnings of Christ's return. Little wonder the Lord compared today's generation to the days of Noah.

Over twenty years ago, Dr. George Wald, scientist at Harvard University and recipient of the Nobel Peace Prize, made this incredibly prophetic statement: "I think human life is threatened as never before in the history of the planet. Not just by one peril, but by many perils that are all working together and coming to a head at about the same time. And that time lies very close to the year 2000. I am one of those scientists who finds it hard to see how the human race is to bring itself much past the year 2000."[2]

It must be stated that no one knows the exact time of Christ's return. In fact, Jesus said, "But of that day and hour knoweth no man, no, not the angels of heaven, but my Father only" (Matt. 24:36). So it is foolish to set dates, but we are assured once the "fig tree buds," that generation will not pass without witnessing the Lord's return.

The "Generation"

In the passage, "This generation shall not pass, till all these things be fulfilled" (Matt. 24:34), the Greek word for "generation" is *genea*, meaning "age, generation, nation, or time."[3] The reference to "generation" seems to have a double meaning, referring to the age who has witnessed Israel become a nation *and* the nation of Israel itself will not pass away until it sees the coming of Christ. Firstly, Scripture is clear that the

Jewish race will never perish: "Thus saith the LORD, which giveth the sun for a light by day, and the ordinances of the moon and of the stars for a light by night, which divideth the sea when the waves thereof roar; The LORD of hosts is his name: If those ordinances depart from before me, saith the LORD, then the seed of Israel also shall cease from being a nation before me for ever" (Jer. 31:35–36). Secondly, in 1998 Israel celebrated its fiftieth year as a nation, and with each passing decade, we continue to witness an acceleration of the prophetical signs as a woman travailing in childbirth. Therefore, Jesus' use of the word "generation" apparently indicated a span of time, and because the Jews *will* witness the return of Christ, it necessarily included a race of people.

How long then is a generation? There are a couple of suggestions. First, Webster defines a generation as "the average span of time between the birth of parents and that of their offsprings," roughly twenty-five years. A second possibility may be around forty years. Scripture says the Israelites, who were led out of Egypt, wandered "in the wilderness forty years, until all the generation, that had done evil in the sight of the LORD, was consumed" (Num. 32:13).

Though the fig tree "became tender" in May of 1948, it actually budded or "put forth its leaves" in the Six-Day War of June 1967 when the Jews captured Jerusalem, regaining control of their beloved city after nearly twenty-six hundred years. This was also a miracle of untold proportion. When we measure forty years from this significant event, it takes us up to the year 2007 as a possible time for Christ's return. As exciting as that is, the thrilling part for the believer is that we are removed at the Rapture seven years *before* the return of Christ, or possibly around the year 2000!

It must be noted there is significance to the repetitive use of numbers in Scripture. The number forty is used more than ninety times. It rained forty days and forty nights when the

Lord destroyed the earth by the flood (Gen. 7:4,12). Moses killed an Egyptian for beating a Hebrew, and then fled from Pharaoh to the land of Midian for forty years before God appeared to him in the burning bush (Exod. 2–3). After Moses led the Israelites out of Egypt, he went into the presence of God on Mount Sinai for forty days and forty nights where he wrote the Ten Commandments (Exod. 34:28). Because of their disobedience and rebellion toward God, the Israelites wandered in the wilderness forty years (Deut. 8:2). David was king of Israel for forty years (2 Sam. 5:4). His son Solomon also reigned over Israel forty years (2 Chron. 9:30). Jesus fasted in the wilderness forty days and forty nights before He began His three-year ministry (Matt. 4:2). And after His crucifixion and resurrection, He remained on the earth forty days before He ascended into a cloud to the Father (Acts 1:3,9). So we see through Scripture a pattern regarding the number forty, and as such, the importance of the number cannot be overlooked.

Other theories have been proposed which also place the Rapture around the year 2000. The apostle Peter wrote, "But, beloved, be not ignorant of this one thing, that one day is with the Lord as a thousand years, and a thousand years as one day" (2 Pet. 3:8). The number seven in the Bible represents completion. From Adam to Abraham was two thousand years, from Abraham to Christ was two thousand years, and from Christ to the present has been nearly two thousand years. After Jesus returns, He will then reign on the earth for a thousand years. These figures total seven thousand years, and may possibly represent the perfect and complete number for humankind's existence.

Again, using the same reference of a day is as a thousand years, in the fifth chapter of Hosea, the prophet records God's words of rebuke toward Israel for their apostasy. He concluded His rebuke with these words: "I will go and return to my place, till they acknowledge their offence, and seek my face: in their affliction they will seek me early" (Hos. 5:15). Israel responded to God's rebuke by saying, "After *two* days will he revive us: in the *third* day he will raise us up, and we shall live in his sight" (Hos. 6:2, emphasis mine). Since Jesus returned to His place with the Father nearly two thousand years ago, possibly representing the two days in this passage, most of the Jews have yet to acknowledge their guilt of apostasy. While they have experienced a steady flow of persecution, the Jews will suffer tremendous affliction during the Tribulation, causing them to seek God's face, just as the passage warns. Their restoration will finally occur at the Second Coming of Christ, where afterward they will "live before Him" during His millennial reign, or possibly as the Scripture states, "the third day." Could the new millennium be the *third* day?

Again, no one knows the exact time, but Israel is the key to unlocking prophecy, and nearly everything regarding the end times directly revolves around her, "the apple of his eye" (Zech. 2:8). Of course, when Jesus answered the disciples' questions on the Mount of Olives, He knew His return would be delayed for thousands of years, but He graciously gave the signs so this generation living in the apostasy of the last days would recognize them and know He is near, thereby "looking for that blessed hope, and the glorious appearing of the great God and our Saviour Jesus Christ" (Titus 2:13).

Jesus listed a number of signs to be watchful for. He warned of the rise of false christs and false prophets, wars and rumors of wars, plagues and famines, earthquakes, as well as terrors and great signs from heaven. Keep in mind, it is the frequency and intensity with which these signs are occurring which herald the imminency of Christ's return. "All these are the beginning of sorrows. . . . So likewise ye, when ye shall see all these things, know that it is near, even at the doors" (Matt. 24:8,33).

False Christs and False Prophets

For many shall come in my name, saying, I am Christ; and
shall deceive many. . . . And many false prophets shall rise,
and shall deceive many.

—Matthew 24:5,11

False christs and false prophets have been around since the beginning of recorded history. Moses warned of them, as did Jeremiah, Ezekiel, the apostle Paul, Peter, and a number of others. In fact, at the time of Christ's birth in Bethlehem, a false christ named Judas, of all things, arose in Galilee and deceived many into following him (Acts 5:37). Today, as the day draws nearer to Jesus' return, we have seen a proliferation of individuals claiming messianic authority. False christs and false prophets have become commonplace newsmakers. As society has increasingly separated from God and His Word, people have steadily become easier targets for deception. It is their unfamiliarity with the Scriptures that is the catalyst to accepting one's claims of messianic authority. Scripture says, "Beware lest any man spoil you through philosophy and vain deceit, after the tradition of men, after the rudiments of the world, and not after Christ" (Col. 2:8). The rise in false christs and false prophets is the direct result of a world which has abandoned Truth. In the last one hundred years, a steady flow of deceivers have surfaced.

Near the turn of the twentieth century, Baha'u'llah, also known as "God's Messenger" and the "Divine Teacher," founded the Baha'i religion, which has a current worldwide following of five million people. Among his many claims, he declared himself to be "the One promised by all religions."

In the 1930s, George Baker, also known as "Father Major Jealous Divine," founded the worldwide Universal Peace Mission Movement. He rose in messianic popularity after a judge, who sentenced him to a year in jail and assessed him a five hundred dollar fine for disturbing the peace, suddenly died. Divine supposedly willed the judge's death because he interfered with his program, and as a result, Father Divine was placed in the spotlight as one possessing the power of God.

But in the past thirty years alone, we have seen a marked increase in this type of deception. As far back as the 1970s, those claiming to be the Messiah include Guruji, Charles Manson, India's Maharaj Ji, Korea's Rev. Sun Myung Moon (who is still active in the nineties and founder of the Unification Church), the Children of God leader Moses David Berg, and Lord Maitreya of the New Age avatars. Perhaps the most notorious of false christs was the People's Temple leader, the Rev. Jim Jones, who regarded himself as the "reincarnation of Jesus Christ." Jones made this chilling statement: "I am peace. I am justice. I am equality. *I am God.*" Tragically, in November of 1978, Jones persuaded over nine hundred of his devoted followers to take their own lives in a mass suicide. Those who refused to drink the cyanide-laced punch were shot to death, including Jim Jones, who was found dead with a gunshot wound to his forehead.

The 1980s saw the rise of Transcendental Meditation leader "His Holiness" Maharishi Mahesh Yogi, whose New Age approach to inner peace has amassed a worldwide following of four million people. There was the late Bhagwan Shree Rajneesh, a guru from India who amassed a following of some 375,000 people worldwide. He chose the name "Bhagwan" because it meant "the embodiment of God."

The 1990s saw the rise of David Koresh, leader of the Branch Davidians in Waco, Texas, referred to by some as the "Latter-Day Lamb." Gabriel of Sedona appeared on NBC's "Dateline" claiming to be Jesus Christ Himself. Marshall Applewhite also claimed messianic authority, Known as "Do," the leader of the Heaven's Gate cult, he and thirty-eight of his followers left their "containers" by committing suicide in March of 1997. They had the misguided hope of catching a spaceship on to heaven, which they believed was following behind the Hale-Bopp comet.

Indeed, Scripture warns in the last days "evil men and seducers shall wax worse and worse, deceiving, and being deceived" (2 Tim. 3:13). We can expect false christs and false prophets to continue until the ultimate deceivers emerge, the Antichrist and his accomplice, the False Prophet.

Wars and Rumors of Wars

And ye shall hear of wars and rumours of wars: see that ye be not troubled: for all these things must come to pass, but the end is not yet. For nation shall rise against nation, and kingdom against kingdom: and there shall be famines, and pestilences, and earthquakes, in divers places.
—Matthew 24:6–7

Wars

It seems peace must be sitting under the pot of gold at the end of the rainbow. We are always pursuing it, but can never find it. Thomas A. Kempis once said, "All men desire peace, but few desire those things that make for peace." Indeed, wars and conflict have raged throughout recorded history, but they have usually concentrated in a single area at a time, that is, until the twentieth century.

In the past thirty years alone, more than sixty conflicts have erupted, occurring simultaneously in various parts of the world. In fact, the constant turmoil drew the attention of "ABC Morning News," which confirmed there has been "continual warfare somewhere on the planet since 1945."[4]

Incredibly, the twentieth century has seen more than two hundred major conflicts worldwide, including the Russo-Japanese War (1904–05); the Balkan wars (1912–13); World War I (1914–18); the Spanish Civil War (1937–39); World War II (1939–45); the Colombian Civil War (1948–53); the Korean War (1950–53); the Vietnam War (1963–73); the Lebanese Civil War (1973–82); the Angolan Civil War (1975–91); the Iran-Iraq War (1980–88); the Afghanistan Civil War (1979–89); the Falklands War (1982); the Gulf War (1991); and the Bosnian conflict (1991–95).[5] Though not long lasting, two highly notable wars in Israel would include the Six-Day War of June 1967, followed by the Yom Kippur War in October of 1973.

Today, there are a number of ongoing conflicts worldwide. These include the Georgian military revolt; the intervention in Lesotho by South Africa and Botswana; the Tutsi Congo revolt; the Saudi-Yemen border conflict; the Yemeni tribal uprising; the Guinea-Bissau Civil War; the Burmese Civil War; the Second Eritrea-Ethiopia War; the Rwandan Civil War; the Burundi Civil War; the Algerian Civil War; the Kashmir War and Indo-Pakistan border conflict; the Indonesian Aceh rebellion; the Kurdish rebellion in Turkey; the Sri Lanka Civil War; the Sierra Leone Civil War; the Northern Ireland conflict; and the crisis in Kosovo.[6]

All of these wars and conflicts combined have claimed the lives of more than seventy million people, making the twentieth century the bloodiest era in human history.

For thousands of years, battles have been fought with basic weaponry—swords and spears, bows and arrows. In the case of David and Goliath, a slingshot and the power of God brought down the giant Philistine (1 Sam. 17:45–49). Likewise, the Spirit of the living God descended on Samson, enabling him to kill a thousand men simply with the jawbone of a donkey (Judg. 15:14–16). But the twentieth century alone has seen the development of conventional, nuclear, biological, and chemical warfare. Their development corresponds with Daniel's prophecy that "knowledge shall be increased" at the end of time (Dan. 12:4).

Ironically, nuclear weapons were introduced just over fifty years ago as a means of *securing peace*. After witnessing detonation of the world's first atomic bomb on July 16, 1945, its inventor, physicist J. Robert Oppenheimer, stated, "I have become Death, the destroyer of worlds"[7] Less than a month later, the people of Hiroshima and Nagasaki, Japan, were the target of his prophetic words. No wonder Solomon wrote, "For in much wisdom is much grief: and he that increaseth knowledge increaseth sorrow" (Eccl. 1:18). And so today, in an effort to secure peace, mankind has compiled enough nuclear weapons to blow the earth all the way to Pluto. But nuclear weapons do incalculable destruction to the earth and its atmosphere, so it was incumbent upon physicists to develop more streamlined weapons of mass destruction. Today, we secure the peace with chemical and biological weapons.

Chemical agents include vesicants which burn or blister the skin of its victims, lung-damaging agents which choke, and blood agents which also cause choking. All of these chemical agents can be dispersed by either artillery shells, mortar shells, rockets, land minds, missiles, aircraft spray, or aircraft bombs.[8] Nerve agents, such as Tabun and Sarin, are among the deadliest of chemical agents. On March 20, 1995, during the morning rush hour, members of the cult Aum Shinri Kyo, or the Supreme Truth, released the nerve agent Sarin into a Tokyo subway system, killing twelve people and injuring thousands.

Biological warfare would include weapons containing viruses, bacteria, or biological toxins. The viruses may include Ebola, the Hanta virus, the Venezuelan Equine encephalitis, causing, respectively, hemorrhagic fever, respiratory distress, and swelling of the brain. Bacterial agents may include Vibrio cholera, causing gastroenteritis, which results in up to one liter of fluids lost per hour; Yersinia pestis, causing lung fever and swollen lymph nodes; and Bacillus anthracis, the causative agent of anthrax, a disease which causes boils on the skin and lesions on the lungs. Biological toxins are extremely potent and include botulinum toxin and Clostridium perfringens. Botulinum toxin produces respiratory paralysis, causing its victims to suffocate. An estimated one gram of botulinum can kill up to ten million people. Clostridium perfringens cause necrotism, or death of the flesh.[9]

As scary as all this sounds, the fact is, these weapons will definitely be used someday during the Tribulation. Scripture warns, "Their flesh shall consume away while they stand upon their feet, and their eyes shall consume away in their holes, and their tongue shall consume away in their mouth" (Zech. 14:12). Scripture also warns "a noisome and grievous sore" (Rev. 16:2) will form on men's skin, a clear indication of radioactivity, or even possibly that of chemical and biological activity.

Countries currently possessing biological and chemical weapons include China, Taiwan, North Korea, Syria, Egypt, Iran, Iraq, Cuba, Israel, the former Soviet states, Japan, and the United States.[10]

Rumors of Wars
The Cuban Missile Crisis is perhaps the most notable rumor of war during this twentieth century. Less than twenty years after detonation of the first nuclear warhead, two of the world's superpowers, the United States and the former Soviet Republic, were locked in a show of force for two weeks in October of 1962. Shortly afterward, Anatoly Gribkov, Soviet Republic and Army Chief of Operations, stated, "Nuclear catastrophe was hanging by a thread . . . and we weren't counting days or hours, but minutes."

More recently, in February of 1998, another rumor of war

occurred as the United States postured against Iraqi leader Saddam Hussein for failing to allow United Nations weapons inspectors to search suspected facilities for the storage of chemical and biological weapons. Again, a standoff ensued between the nations, heightened by Russian president Boris Yeltsin's threat to intervene on Iraq's behalf if the U.S. acted on its threats. Finally, United Nations Secretary–General Kofi Annan stepped up and initiated discussions with Saddam Hussein, who then relented at the eleventh hour.

In May of 1998, yet another nuclear crisis arose. Rumors of wars were flying in South Asia as a result of India's underground detonation of five sub-kiloton nuclear warheads. Understandably feeling threatened, neighboring Pakistan followed suit with the underground detonation of five of their own nuclear warheads. India and Pakistan have been longstanding rivals, having engaged in two conflicts since 1947. Today, the neighboring countries are engaged in heated discussions regarding drug trafficking and the rise of alleged Pakistani state-sponsored terrorists settling into the Indian regions of Jammu and Kashmir. If the matter is not resolved, the situation could potentially escalate into a serious conflict.

As history is often destined to repeat itself, in November of 1998, Saddam Hussein once again refused to allow inspectors from the United Nations Special Commission (UNSCOM) to search suspected facilities for the storage of chemical and biological weapons used during the Iran-Iraq War in the 1980s. This time, Iraqis vowed not to back down to threats of air strikes from the United States, and other Arab leaders urged Saddam Hussein to relent. In his refusal, the necessary troops and machinery were deployed to the region, and once again, Hussein relented at the eleventh hour. Albert Einstein once said, "Every kind of peaceful cooperation among men is primarily based on mutual trust." The United States' victory in the standoff seems a hollow one, as Saddam Hussein continually demonstrates his inability to be trusted.

At the close of World War II, General Douglas MacArthur made this chilling statement: "Men since the beginning of time have sought peace . . . military alliances, balances of power, leagues of nations all in turn failed, leaving the only path to be by way of the crucible of war. We have had our last chance. If we do not now despise some greater and more equitable system, Armageddon will be at our door."[11]

Unfortunately, wars and rumors of wars will continue, and there will be no peace on earth until Jesus returns at the battle of Armageddon and thereafter sets up His righteous millennial kingdom. In the meantime, the peace men search for can only be found in Jesus Christ. In fact, He said, "In me ye might have peace. In the world ye shall have tribulation: but be of good cheer; I have overcome the world" (John 16:33).

Finally, in the Valley of Megiddo in Israel, all the nations of the world will gather for the battle of Armageddon (Rev. 16:14,16). However, it will not be the last conflict for mankind. Scripture reveals a final war at the conclusion of the Millennium (Rev. 20:7–9).

Plagues and Famines

. . . in divers places . . . famines, and pestilences. . . .
—**Luke 21:11**

Plagues

Plagues and famines have been around since the days of the Israelites. But today, we are not only witnessing the return of diseases once considered eradicated, we are seeing new strains of infectious diseases that make the plagues of Egypt look like ants at a picnic. In fact, infectious diseases are the leading cause of death worldwide and were the third cause of death in the United States in 1992.[12] As the day draws near for the return of Christ, we are seeing the steady increase of plagues, just as Jesus predicted.

In 1979, the first case of Acquired Immune Deficiency Syndrome (AIDS) was reported. By the end of 1997, a staggering 11.7 million people had died worldwide from the disease, and more than 30.6 million are now living with AIDS or HIV, the human immunodeficiency virus which causes AIDS.[13] What's more, current figures show an estimated sixteen thousand people a day are contracting the deadly virus for which there is still no cure. This disease is no longer considered an epidemic, but a pandemic.

Cholera, malaria, and tuberculosis were once controlled, but have made a strong comeback in recent years. In January of 1991, an epidemic of cholera broke out in South America and quickly spread to other countries, claiming thousands of lives. Without treatment, severe cases of cholera can result in death within hours.[14] Malaria, once the leading cause of death around the world, was considered eradicated by the 1960s. Today, malaria infects more than 270 million people worldwide, killing more than two million each year.[15] In the early 1990s, an outbreak of malaria was reported in New Jersey, New York, and Texas.[16] Tuberculosis is on the decrease in the United States, but in March of 1998, the World Health Organization announced that tuberculosis has again become a major global problem, with one billion people likely to become infected and seventy million to die within the next twenty years.[17]

Dengue and dengue hemorrhagic fever have reemerged throughout the world, with more than one hundred million cases of dengue and hundreds of thousands of dengue hemorrhagic fever reported annually.[18] It is a mosquito-borne viral disease comparable to malaria. After a lengthy absence, dengue fever has also resurfaced in the United States.

We have further seen the emergence of the Ebola virus, first detected in Africa in 1976; the food-borne bacteria *E. coli*, first traced to hamburger meat in 1982; the Hanta virus, transmitted by diseased rats, which first appeared in the Four Corners region of the United States in May of 1993; an outbreak of monkeypox in the Congo beginning in February of 1996; and a terrifying strain of flesh-eating bacteria which surfaced in the mid-nineties. In April of 1997, the World Health Organization announced "at least thirty new infectious diseases, with no known treatment, cure, or vaccine, have emerged in the past twenty years." This is just as the Lord said it would be prior to His return to earth.

Famines

In the twentieth century, widespread famine began in the 1970s as a result of the population explosion. Experts have calculated that it took from the *beginning of time* to A.D. 1850, for the world population to reach one billion. But from 1850 to 1930, the population grew exponentially, reaching its second billion. From 1930 to 1960, just thirty short years, we reached our third billion. From 1960 to 1975, in only fifteen years, the world population grew to four billion.[19]

And now just past the year 2000, we have nearly six billion people on the planet. Unfortunately, most countries are not able to produce the food needed to feed their own citizens and rely heavily on other nations to supply their food. But changing global weather patterns, causing drought, severe flooding, and a number of other environmental factors, have led to disastrous crop failures and an overall shortage of food production, making it exceedingly difficult to feed an ever-growing world population. In fact, in the United States, the world's breadbasket, food reserves of grain and corn are at their lowest levels in sixteen years, while wheat reserves are at its lowest level in nearly fifty years, yet we continually reach into our supply to meet the needs of the starving in other countries. The global situation is critical.

Famine can also be a man-made peril, the direct result of war. Raging conflicts create an inability to distribute food, and millions face starvation. Since the 1970s, Asia and Africa have continually been plagued by famine due to drought and warring factions. Hundreds of thousands of people died of starvation in Cambodia in the late seventies. In the mid-eighties, nearly a million people starved to death in Ethiopia. In the early nineties, famine killed hundreds of thousands in Somalia.

Today, the African continent remains in desperate need of food relief. In Ethiopia, eight hundred thousand people are starving due to drought and a poor harvest. The war-torn Sudanese nation is experiencing famine. According to the United Nations World Food Programme, 2.6 million people are currently at risk of starvation, while 1.5 million have already died.[20]

In the Philippines, severe drought has caused a shortage of food production, leaving three hundred thousand in need of food. North Korea is suffering a critical famine as well. To date, an estimated three million people have died of starvation,[21] and nearly five million are malnourished, subsisting on six hundred calories a day or less. A two-million-ton shortfall in grain production due to drought and flooding, combined with communist mismanagement, are all factors in the crisis.[22]

Drought conditions in Russia have also created a tremendous crisis. Russia is expected to harvest a scant fifty-two million tons of grain this year, hardly enough to sustain the country through the winter months. It is their worst crop since the 1950s. The United States has proposed a five hundred million dollar support package, to include 1.5 million tons of wheat, along with 1.5 million tons of meat, provided

Moscow promises to distribute the aid fairly.[23]

As if all this were not devastating enough, there is a terrible three and one-half–year drought on the horizon at the commencement of the Tribulation (Rev. 11:2,6).

Earthquakes

... and earthquakes, in divers places.

—Matthew 24:7

Earthquakes are one of the most frightening catastrophes known to man. They strike without warning, destroying lives and communities in a matter of minutes. These, too, are nothing new to this generation. In fact, major earthquakes have been recorded throughout history, their story carved on everything from cave walls to pyramids. Scripture itself records four earthquakes, including the severe quake which occurred at the resurrection of Jesus (Matt. 28:2). But some would have us to believe the number of earthquakes we are experiencing today is unchanged from the beginning of time; the only difference being advanced seismic technology to better monitor the earth's movement. Certainly geologists can more accurately track earthquakes today, but even *since* the development of this technology, there has been an enormous increase in seismic activity.

The World Almanac contains a listing of major earthquakes, measure 5.5 or greater on the Richter scale, that have occurred worldwide since A.D. 526. From that year to A.D. 856, over a three hundred thirty-year period, there were only two major earthquakes. The next major earthquake occurred two hundred years later, in A.D. 1057. From that time to A.D. 1900, nearly eight hundred fifty years, there were a total of twenty-one major earthquakes, with ten- to thirty-year gaps in between when seismic activity was relatively quiet.[24]

The twentieth century changed all that. From 1900 to 1950, there were *twenty-one* major earthquakes recorded, averaging two to four years apart. Incredibly, from 1950 to 1998, there were an astounding *ninety-three* major earthquakes. Those occurring from 1950 to 1960 were about three years apart; from 1960 to 1970, two years apart; from 1970 to 1980, one year; from 1980 to 1990, six months to a year; with the decade of the 1990s showing the most startling figures yet. From 1990 to 1995, there were as many as four major earthquakes a *year*. And in one year's time alone, from July 1996 to July 1997, there were *twenty-six* major earthquakes worldwide.[25] The first four months alone of 1998 witnessed twenty-four major earthquakes![26]

In 1973, the U.S. Geological Survey, a branch of the Department of the Interior, established the National Earthquake Information Center (NEIC). The NEIC provides rapid reports of seismic activity to scientists and governmental agencies throughout the world, as well as the general public. It has an extensive seismic database, with more than three thousand national and international reporting networks stationed in some eighty countries, making it *the* premier information center in the United States for earthquake data retrieval. According to the NEIC, there are "many millions" of earthquakes occurring every year measuring 4.5 or less on the Richter scale.[27]

Though the world has never experienced shaking to the degree it will soon, some of the most devastating earthquakes have certainly left their indelible marks. On March 27, 1964, at 5:36 p.m., the earth shook for nearly four minutes beneath Anchorage, Alaska, in what is the longest recorded earthquake in U.S. history. Measuring an astonishing 8.6 on the Richter scale, this geologic catastrophe cut a five hundred-mile path of destruction, creating fissures in the earth as wide as thirty feet. The quake released energy equivalent to twelve thousand Hiroshima-type atomic bombs, or two hundred forty tones of TNT. It heaved one hundred square miles of the earth's surface upward, resulting in the "greatest area of vertical displacement ever measured in earthquake history."[28] It sent shock waves thousands of miles. Incredibly, the ground beneath Houston, Texas, momentarily raised four inches from the radiating waves.[29]

When the earth finally stopped shaking, one hundred thirty-one lives were lost, many of whom were never found, and twenty-five thousand square miles of land had been moved from its place. Anchorage was moved six feet toward the sea, while neighboring Valdez moved thirty-three feet, and Seward, forty-seven. The force of the quake caused the entire planet to shake for two more weeks, though the aftershocks around Anchorage were felt for eighteen months, as the ground continued to quake more than ten thousand times.[30]

As powerful as the Alaskan earthquake was, it will pale in comparison to the reeling of the earth at the end of the Tribulation. At that time, there will be "a great earthquake, such as was not since men were upon the earth, so mighty an earthquake, and so great. . . . And every island fled away, and the mountains were not found" (Rev. 16:18,20).

Terrors and Great Signs in the Heavens

. . . in divers places . . . fearful sights and great signs shall there be from heaven.

—Luke 21:11

Three different heavens may be seen in Scripture. The first heaven is the air we breathe, the space around us and above us where birds fly and airplanes soar. The second is the celestial heaven or the universe with its stars, planets, and galaxies. The third heaven is the home of God.

Weather

One could scarcely imagine the intense changing weather patterns and subsequent calamities that have befallen this decade. Floods, hurricanes, typhoons, droughts abound. Meteorologists have placed the blame on El Niño, a warm weather pattern that builds in the Pacific Ocean over a period of months. What causes it is still a mystery, but scientists could possibly find a clue in the name. Peruvian fishermen gave the name "El Niño" to a weather system that appeared every year around Christmas. "El Niño" refers to "the Christ child," and all this unusual weather is a sign from Him to the world that He is near, "even at the door."

The weather has been erratic for the past thirty years, but the 1990s have been unprecedented. In the last eight years, there have been twelve occasions of destructive tornadoes sweeping the U.S., five major cyclones hitting Asia; another five typhoons hitting Asia and the Philippines; eleven tropical storms and a monsoon hitting the Caribbean, the U.S., and Mexico; four Siberian-type blizzards and an ice storm hitting the U.S., with seven worldwide volcanic eruptions and nineteen states in the U.S. experiencing record-breaking temperatures since 1980, including Arizona's blistering one hundred twenty-eight degrees set on June 29, 1994.[31] And in a year's time, from 1996 to 1997, there were "as many as 8,000 national disasters" in the U.S.[32]

Since 1995, there have been twenty-eight hurricanes, including Hurricane Bonnie in August of 1998 which did over one billion dollars in damage. And in September of 1998, for the first time in over a century, since 1892, four hurricanes, namely, Karl, Georges, Ivan, and Jeanne, occurred simultaneously in the Atlantic Ocean. According to meteorologist Michele Huber at the National Hurricane Center in Miami, "This is definitely something beyond the ordinary."[33]

In the last week of October 1998, Hurricane Mitch

slammed into Central America with winds over one hundred eighty miles an hour, killing more than ten thousand people and making it one of the deadliest Atlantic storms on record. The hurricane dumped as much as two feet of rain a day, causing thousands to be killed in mud slides alone. And to compound matters, the Cerro Negro volcano in Nicaragua erupted, spewing lava, hot gas, and flaming rocks down on the devastated region.[34]

And what of all the flooding? From A.D. 1228 to A.D. 1900, over six hundred seventy years, there were only five major floods or tidal waves recorded. In less than one hundred years, since the beginning of the twentieth century, there have been ninety major floods worldwide, fifty-six of them occurring since 1970.[35]

A recent article in *Life* magazine stated, "Since the beginning of 1997, more than 16,000 have been killed worldwide by the weather and nearly $50 billion in damage has been done. In the U.S., the figures are 456 dead and $13 billion lost. While there have been cataclysms of great immensity and intensity in our century, the distribution, variety and frequency of the recent rotten weather has been extraordinary."[36]

In July of 1998, meteorologists officially declared the El Niño weather pattern over, but as we have already seen, more surprises await. Scripture warns, "there shall be signs in the sun, and in the moon, and in the stars; and upon the earth distress of nations, with perplexity; the sea and the waves roaring; Men's hearts failing them for fear, and for looking after those things which are coming on the earth: for the powers of heaven shall be shaken" (Luke 21:25–26).

Unexplained Phenomena

"In the beginning God created the heaven and the earth" (Gen. 1:1). "For by him were *all* things created, that are in heaven, and that are in earth, visible and invisible, whether they be thrones, or dominions, or principalities, or powers: *all* things were created by him, and for him" (Col. 1:16, emphasis mine).

That means everything—dinosaurs, Bigfoot, Sasquatch, Yeti, the Boggy Creek monster, the Loch Ness monster, the Bermuda Triangle, Atlantis, poltergeists, UFOs, and whatever else there may be out there. Try as we might, there are some things we are just not going to know about. But God knows everything. He is in control of all things; and nothing happens that He does not allow.

Because Jesus is about to return, the god of this world, Satan, and all his minions are working overtime to deceive people into believing anything but the truth. As believers, we know "the truth is in Jesus" (Eph. 4:21), and no matter what we see with our eyes, if it conflicts with the Scriptures, it is a lie from the devil, sent to confuse and distort the truth. The apostle Paul warned of this. "Now the Spirit speaketh expressly, that in the latter times some shall depart from the faith, giving heed to seducing spirits, and doctrines of devils" (1 Tim. 4:1).

Over the past thirty years, we have seen an explosion of unexplained phenomena. There have been millions of UFO sightings around the world, with thousands of people claiming alien abduction. Of course, Hollywood has pounced on all the fascination with the unknown by bombarding us with television shows like "Star Trek"; "The X-Files"; "Millennium"; "Sightings"; "Alien Nation"; "Earth: Final Conflict"; Fox's "Alien Autopsy"; "Third Rock from the Sun"; and "Roswell: The UFO Cover-Up," as well as movies like *Independence Day; ET; Enemy Mine; Star Trek: The Movie; Star Wars; Close Encounters of the Third Kind; Men in Black; 2001: A Space Odyssey; Contact*, and the list goes on and on.

It is not a coincidence that we are seeing all this heightened alien and UFO activity at this crucial time before Jesus returns. It is essential to the end-time scenario so that when the Rapture happens, there can be a satisfactory explanation for the hundreds of millions of persons who have disappeared. Let us consider some of this groundwork.

In March of 1997, in a suburb outside of San Diego, California, thirty-nine members of the Heaven's Gate cult took their own lives in an effort to get on board what they believed was a spaceship bound for heaven following behind the Hale-Bopp comet. With all its haunting pictures and details, this tragedy got enormous media attention and actually set the stage for the eventual explanation of the Rapture.

Then, in December of 1997, members of the cult God's Salvation Church began gathering in Garland, Texas, to await God's arrival in a spaceship on March 31, 1998. He didn't show.

In January of 1998, in Madrid, Spain, a thirty-member sect linked with the Solar Temple cult attempted to commit suicide, also believing they would be carried away by a spaceship from the summit of Tenerife's Teide volcano. Fortunately, the police intervened as cult members were staging their "last supper" at a private home. In 1994, however, seventy-four members of the Solar Temple cult did commit suicide.

Finally, in March of 1998, again in Garland, Texas, a one hundred fifty-member Taiwanese sect, led by Hon-Ming Chen, claimed that God would appear just after midnight on Channel 18, of any United States television set, to announce His plans for the following week. Chen and his followers believed God was going to descend to earth to take hundreds of millions of people to another planet by, what else, flying saucers in order to save us from a nuclear holocaust in 1999.

Because the Rapture is so close, all these events are acts of demonic deception, clearly orchestrated in order to provide an acceptable answer to the whereabouts of millions of missing people. The proliferation of UFO sightings and the unexplained phenomena are all part of an agenda God is permitting for the end times. Scripture says, "And I will shew wonders in heaven above, and signs in the earth beneath" (Acts 2:19).

Another plausible explanation for the disappearance of millions may be attributed to the cosmos. On August 27, 1998, the most powerful energy burst ever detected from beyond the solar system struck the earth over the Pacific Ocean. For five minutes, "It was as if night was briefly turned into day in the ionosphere," states Umran Inan of Stanford University. A neutron star, known as a magnetar, burst about twenty thousand light years away in the earth's galaxy, the Milky Way. The star's magnetic field is billions of times stronger than anything on earth and one hundred times stronger than any previously discovered in the universe. It did not come closer than thirty miles from the earth's surface, but researchers have identified this event as the first occasion a significant change has occurred in the earth's environment due to energy released from a distant star. According to Robert Duncan of the University of Texas, "a magnet this strong could erase the magnetic strip on the credit cards in your wallet or pull the keys out of your pocket from a distance halfway to the moon."[37] Perhaps some will suggest it could even pull people off the planet.

Consider the comet Shoemaker-Levy 9, which in July 1994 collided with the planet Jupiter, releasing more energy into Jupiter's atmosphere than all of the world's nuclear arsenal combined. The collision of a large comet with a planet is considered an extraordinary, millennial event.[38]

Further, on November 7, 1998, satellite companies the world over braced themselves for the most intense Leonid meteor storm in over thirty years as the earth passed through the debris of the Temple-Tuttle comet. The small, dust-like particles of the comet entered the earth's atmosphere at about 155,000 miles an hour and then burned up, but they nonetheless posed a threat of striking any one of the six hundred satellites orbiting the earth which broadcast television shows and transmit pagers and cell phones.[39]

No doubt there has been heightened anxiety over comets and asteroids hitting the earth, with scientists confirming the likelihood of such an occurrence someday. Movies like *Deep Impact, Asteroid,* and *Armageddon* have also contributed to the fear of being obliterated from space.

The truth of the matter is, no comets or asteroids are likely to hit the earth, but within the five-year period from 1998 to 2003, more than eighty comets are expected to pass by. With the Rapture so close, it will seem a plausible explanation to suggest the missing are in spaceships following behind one or any number of these comets. Again, nothing happens that God does not permit, and strange or once-in-a-lifetime events we seem to keep experiencing in our lifetime will ultimately play a part in the end-time agenda as an explanation for the Rapture. All the UFO activity, as well as the neutron stars and comets, are part of the "wonders in heaven above" surrounding the last days.

And what of the "signs in the earth beneath"? Since 1973, there have been more than nine thousand documented cases of crop circle formations on the earth, ninety percent of which have been in England. Colin Andrews, founder and president of Circles Phenomenon Research International, recently interviewed Col. Philip J. Corso (Ret.), who stated, "Crop circles are known to be real by the U.S. government."[40] Andrews became interested in the phenomenon in 1983 after viewing a field containing five circles which were aligned in the shape of a cross.

When the circles first appeared, the magnitude of the situation was so inexplicable that to avert a public panic, the British government and the CIA fabricated a story of two elderly men named Doug and Dave who had nothing better to do in the wee hours of the morning than to pull off an incredible hoax. It was later discovered that the two men were paid to perpetuate the story.

In fact, it is not humanly possible to fabricate a perfect crop circle formation. Crop circles are of extremely complex Euclidian geometry. After their formation, there is an increase of infrared output in and around the new formation. There is an altered magnetic structure, which causes a failure in compasses to point north, the failure of watches and cameras to operate, as well as equipment failure on aircraft flying over the formation. The air within the formation is also disturbed, causing Geiger counters to record higher levels of radiation and voltameters to read higher and lower levels of electricity. Animals are extremely agitated hours before a formation appears, and car batteries in entire villages have failed to operate the morning after a formation is found.[41]

What's more, the unexplained phenomenon has driven farmers, the military, scientists, and untold numbers of enthusiasts into the fields to catch a glimpse of whatever is causing these geometrical figures. Yet even with all the top surveillance equipment, including high-tech laser devices, crop circles just "appear" out of nowhere.[42]

Again, all this unexplained phenomena is a master work of deception, orchestrated by "seducing spirits" (1 Tim. 4:1) at this critical time in order to convince the masses of the existence of extraterrestrial life. Make no mistake, *Christians* are the only aliens in this land, and when Jesus comes to take us to heaven, we are not going in spaceships.

The Days of Lot

And as it was in the days of Noe, so shall it be also in the days of the Son of man. They did eat, they drank, they married wives, they were given in marriage, . . . Likewise also as it was in the days of Lot; they did eat, they drank, they bought, they sold, they planted, they builded.

—**Luke 17:26–28**

Jesus not only compared the generation who would witness His return to that of Noah's day, but He also compared it to the days of Lot. Today, we are witnessing the fulfillment of these prophetic words. Since the early 1970s, homosexual men and women have been petitioning the courts and state legislators to pass laws recognizing same-sex unions. While this remains a hotbed of controversy in the United States, an increasing number of countries are currently recognizing same-sex unions.

Not surprisingly, in 1989, Denmark became the first country to legalize gay marriages, and today there are more than four thousand recorded unions. In 1991, Norway became the second country to legalize gay marriages, followed by Sweden and Hungary in 1995. Also in 1995, six cities in Spain began recognizing same-sex unions, including Barcelona, as well as ninety Dutch towns in the Netherlands. Finland, Slovenia, Iceland, and the Czech Republic are expected to follow suit.

As of this writing, Vermont has a type of legal same-sex union that is recognized by the state, but stops short of recognizing it as a traditional marriage. Hawaii recently refused to legalize same-sex marriages to the surprise of many. It may be, however, only a matter of time until more pressure is brought to bear to go even farther than Vermont in certain other states.

Meanwhile, in San Francisco, Mayor Willie Brown and several city officials attended a civic wedding ceremony uniting fifty same-sex couples in March of 1998. Two years prior, one hundred sixty-three same-sex couples exchanged vows in a domestic partners ceremony. Under the domestic partners ordinance adopted by San Francisco in the early 1990s, same-sex couples can register their committed unions with the city. Since then, more than three thousand couples have registered. To date, however, the state of California has not recognized any of these unions as legal.

The Condition of the Human Race

This know also, that in the last days perilous times shall come. For men shall be lovers of their own selves, covetous, boasters, proud, blasphemers, disobedient to parents, unthankful, unholy, Without natural affection, trucebreakers, false accusers, incontinent, fierce, despisers of those that are good, Traitors, heady, highminded, lovers of pleasures more than lovers of God; Having a form of godliness, but denying the power thereof: from such turn away.
—2 Timothy 3:1–5

In 1990, authors Peter Kim and James Patterson conducted the largest national survey of private morals ever undertaken in any nation. The survey was done in order to assess the level of personal ethics, values, and beliefs in America. In every region of the United States, respondents agreed to answer over eighteen hundred questions truthfully, with the guarantee of total anonymity. The shocking results were published in their book, *The Day America Told the Truth* (Prentice Hall Press, 1991).

Of those responding, ninety-three percent said *they* determine their *own* moral values; eighty-four percent said they would violate the established rules of their religion; and eighty-one percent said they had violated a law because they felt it was wrong in their own view.[43] It was determined that seventy–seven percent of the respondents failed to see the point in observing the Sabbath; seventy-four percent would steal from someone if they thought the item would not be missed; sixty-four percent would lie about a specific matter if it does not cause any harm, while ninety-one percent lie regularly; fifty-six percent said they would drink and drive; fifty-three percent said they would commit adultery; and forty-one percent acknowledged recreational drug use.[44]

When Americans were questioned what they would do for ten million dollars, two-third responded they would: abandon their entire family (twenty-five percent); abandon their church (twenty-five percent); become prostitutes for a week or more (twenty-three percent); give up their American citizenship (sixteen percent); leave their spouses (sixteen percent); withhold testimony and let a murderer go free (ten percent); kill a stranger (seven percent); change their race (six percent); have a sex-change operation (four percent); and put their children up for adoption (three percent).[45]

When it came to matters of spirituality, only ten percent believed in all of the Ten Commandments, and forty percent believed in five or less. Six out of seven people felt it was okay not to believe in God. Yet forty-six percent felt they were going to heaven and only four percent felt they were going to hell.[46] I wonder where the other fifty percent think they are going.

Finally, by the end of 1996, the United States, a nation once founded on Christian principles, had nearly 1.2 million people locked up in federal and state penitentiaries for crime, more than three thousand of whom are awaiting the death penalty.[47]

We hardly need statistics to confirm the endless depth of human depravity. One need only watch daytime talk shows and the evening news. The condition of the human race is precisely as the apostle Paul said it would be prior to the Lord's return.

Travel and Technology

. . . even to the time of the end: many shall run to and fro,
and knowledge shall be increased.

—**Daniel 12:4**

Travel

In this passage, the Hebrew word *shuwt* is used, meaning "to lash, i.e., the sea with oars, to row; by implication, to travel."[48] Man has traveled by boat for thousands of years. In fact, we know nearly eight hundred years before Christ's incarnation that Jonah "found a ship going to Tarshish" (Jon. 1:3). But when it came to traveling by land, man has not been quite so innovative.

For almost six thousand, years travel across land had either been on foot or on the backs of animals. Over the years, there were some good transportational ideas, amounting to chariots in ancient times, leading up to stagecoaches and covered wagons in the 1800s. But as fast as this was, compared to traveling on foot, it was still not fast enough. So beginning in the early 1800s, attention was given to developing faster forms of travel, and by the end of that century, trains had become the main source of transportation, with automobiles just beginning to emerge. There were even some fanatics who believed we could travel by air, of all things, which posed quite a challenge.

But on December 17, 1903, Orville and Wilbur Wright made a breakthrough. Near Kitty Hawk, North Carolina, the two brothers flew the first motorized plane to ever carry a human being. They each flew two flights, with the longest distance measuring eight hundred fifty-two feet and lasting a total of fifty-nine seconds.[49]

Today, in as little as a hundred years, modes of travel have been mastered. We cross the oceans in cruise ships weighing literally one hundred thousand tons and reaching as high as fourteen-story buildings. In Europe, commuters can cross the land in trains reaching speeds in excess of three hundred miles an hour. Vehicles of every shape, size, and color enable us to get anywhere at any time. And aviation has improved more than slightly since Orville and Wilbur's days. Jets and airbuses take us around the world in a matter of hours. Nearly seventy million people a year travel out of Chicago's O'Hare Airport, the busiest airport in the United States, while London's Heathrow Airport is the busiest internationally, with nearly sixty million worldwide travelers a year.[50]

Indeed, the twentieth century has seen traveling to and fro, just as the prophet Daniel predicted.

Technology

John the apostle wrote, "And there are also many other things which Jesus did, the which, if they should be written every one, I suppose that even the world itself could not contain the books that should be written. Amen" (John 21:25).

In the same way, it is certainly impossible for any one book to contain, let alone detail, the explosion of knowledge and technology the twentieth century has seen. Whatever was invented before this century has certainly been perfected, and there is nothing of which my mind can conceive that mankind does not have at its disposal. At the end of the nineteenth century, someone said, "All that can be invented has been invented." And here we are at the end of the twentieth century, and for the life of me, I cannot imagine what remains to be invented. We can see where things will be perfected, but what is there that man does not already have?

Medical advancement has gone through the roof. Recently, in Houston, Texas, a young boy miraculously survived a tragedy in which ninety-nine percent of his body was burned. Doctors found an area the size of a postage stamp on his heel that had not been burned. They removed it and sent it to a laboratory where they have already reproduced over half of the boy's skin which will eventually be grafted back onto his body.

We can even choose the sex and features of our unborn children by selecting various chromosomal DNA and injecting them into a fertilized egg to be placed into a woman's uterus. Animals have been cloned, and but for the bureaucratic red tape, it is likely the technology would already have been used on humans. In November of 1998, a chilling discovery was made in cloning technology. Scientists are now able to fuse human and animal cells together, with the possible result of creating a human-animal species. Their intent, however, is to grow organs for transplant use.

In this century, we have gone from learning to fly, to placing a man on the moon only a few short decades ago, to making routine trips into outer space so astronauts can do repairs to satellites or even dock and live on space stations for months. We have vessels which can take us to the bottom of the sea where the pressure alone could flatten a man to the width of paper. At the beginning of the twentieth century, it took weeks to get information around the globe, but today we witness events live on television from anyplace on the planet or send instantaneous messages all over the world via the Internet.

In 1876, Alexander Graham Bell invented the telephone. On January 25, 1915, he made the first transcontinental telephone call. From New York, he phoned Thomas A. Watson in San Francisco.[51] Today, we can talk to anyone around the world at any time of the day or night with such clarity in the connection we feel as though we are only rooms apart.

We can simulate reality by virtual reality. We can reach into an endless well of information through the World Wide Web. Computers can do absolutely anything you want them to do. In fact, they can perform a function faster than you can blink. Does anyone even ask how things work anymore?

It is impossible to adequately detail all the accomplishments of the twentieth century, but suffice it to say, the knowledge explosion fulfills Daniel's words regarding the condition of the human race at the time of the end.

In summation, all of these signs have been given so that the generation which would witness them occurring *simultaneously* would know that the Lord Jesus is about to return, yes, He is even "at the door."

Behold, I have told you before.

—Matthew 24:25

Endnotes

1. Mark Twain, as quoted from the World's Greatest Library, in *Apocalypse Next*, William R. Goetz (Horizon Books, Camp Hill, Pennsylvania, 1996), p. 81.
2. Hal Lindsey, *The 1980s: Countdown to Armageddon* (Bantam Books, New York, 1980), p. 17.
3. Spiros Zodhiates, Th.D., ed., *Hebrew-Greek Key Study Bible, King James Version* (World Bible Publishers, 1991), *Dictionary of the Greek Testament*, James Strong, S.T.D., L.L.D., No. 1074, p. 20.
4. William R. Goetz, *Apocalypse Next*, p. 35.
5. Ibid., p. 261.
6. R. Lee, "New and Recent Conflicts of the World," http://www.historyguy.com/new_and_recent_conflicts.html (1998).
7. Rod Olsen Research Services, "Research Trials, Triumphs and Tragedies," Miller D, Miller I, Miller J, and Miller M. The Cambridge Dictionary of Scientists, (Cambridge University Press, Cambridge, UK, 1996).
8. NATO Manual FM8-285-Part I, Chapters 1–6.
9. Scott D. McCulloch, "Biological Warfare and the Implications of Biotechnology," CalPoly Institute Seminar.
10. Ibid.
11. As quoted by Hal Lindsey, *The 1980s: Countdown to Armageddon*, p. 24.
12. National Center for Infectious Diseases, Centers for Disease Control and Prevention, Atlanta, Georgia, May 28, 1997.
13. "Report on the Global HIV/AIDS Epidemic," UNAIDS and the World Health Organization, November 26, 1997.
14. "Cholera Prevention," National Center for Infectious Diseases, Centers for Disease Control and Prevention, Atlanta, Georgia, August 9, 1996.
15. Hal Lindsey, *Planet Earth—2000 A.D.* (Western Front, Ltd., Palos Verdes, California, 1994), pp. 114–115.

16. Jane R. Zucker, M.D., "Changing Patterns of Autochthonous Malaria Transmission in the United States: A Review of Recent Outbreaks," Centers for Disease Control and Prevention, Atlanta, Georgia, January–March 1996.

17. Source: MSNBC.

18. "Information on Dengue Fever and Dengue Hemorrhagic Fever," Division of Vector-Borne Infectious Diseases, National Center for Infectious Diseases, Centers for Disease Control and Prevention, March 1998.

19. *The World Almanac and Book of Facts 1998* (K-III Reference Corporation, 1997), p. 553.

20. CNN Report, July 16, 1998.

21. Source: Reuters.

22. Source: MSNBC.

23. Source: Reuters.

24. *The World Almanac and Book of Facts 1998*, p. 269.

25. Ibid., pp. 269–270.

26. National Earthquake Information Center, U.S. Geologic Survey.

27. Fact Sheet 125-97, National Earthquake Information Center, U.S. Geologic Survey.

28. Quoted from Bruce A. Bolt., *Earthquakes* (W. H. Freeman and Company, New York, 1993), p. 11.

29. Bryce Walker, *Planet Earth—Earthquakes* (Time-Life Books, Alexandria, Virginia, 1982), pp. 18–35.

30. Ibid.

31. *The World Almanac and Books of Facts 1998*, pp. 180, 268, 588–589; FEMA–Reference Library: Disaster Archives.

32. American Red Cross.

33. Lowe's Storm '98 Hurricane Central: Latest Reports; www.storm98.com.

34. Source: Reuters.

35. CNN; *The World Almanac and Books of Facts 1998*, p. 269.

36. Kenneth Miller, "Weather," *Life* magazine, August 1998.

37. Kathy Sawyer, *Washington Post*, September 30, 1998, p. A-01.

38. NASA, Jet Propulsion Laboratory.

39. Source: Reuters.

40. Colin Andrews, Circles Phenomenon Research International, Branford, Connecticut.

41. Colin Andrews, "The Crop Circular," Circles Phenomenon Research International, Branford, Connecticut.

42. Ibid.

43. James Patterson, Peter Kim, *The Day America Told the Truth* (Prentice Hall Press, 1991), p. 27.

44. Ibid., pp. 25–26.

45. Ibid., p. 66.

46. Ibid., pp. 200–201.

47. "Prison Population: Bureau of Justice Statistics," U.S. Department of Justice, December 31, 1996.

48. Spiros Zodhiates, Th.D., ed., *Hebrew-Greek Key Study Bible, King James Version* (World Bible Publishers, 1991), *Dictionary of the Greek Testament*, James Strong, S.T.D., L.L.D., No. 1074, p. 113.

49. *The World Almanac and Book of Facts 1998*, p. 176

50. Ibid., pp. 174–175.

51. Ibid., p. 502.

. . . I will come again, and receive you unto myself; that where I am, there ye may be also.

—John 14:3

Chapter 4

The Rapture of the Church

B EFORE THE SEVEN-YEAR Tribulation begins, the Church, or the body of Christ, will be removed from the earth. By the "Church," we mean all who have sincerely invited Jesus into their hearts, those who truly have a relationship with Him. There are many professing Christians who never "bring forth therefore fruits meet for repentance" (Matt. 3:8). They come to church on Sunday but do little, of anything, for the kingdom of God. They profess Christ with their mouths but not with their lives.

When someone has a true born-again experience, their life changes by the power of the Holy Spirit. There is no exception. No one comes to know the Lord, "rather are known of God" (Gal 4:9), and remain in the condition they were before their profession of faith. That is not to say they will not sin or struggle with old sinful behavior, just as the apostle Paul did (Rom. 7:14–25), but there is a point at which all genuine believers can look back and identify when change began. Scripture is clear that "by works a man is justified, and not by faith only" (Jam. 2:24). Indeed, faith alone saves, but the faith that saves is not alone. Righteousness evidenced by good works *must* accompany faith if there be genuine salvation. "Was not Abraham our father justified by works, when he had offered Isaac his son upon the altar? . . . Likewise also was not Rahab the harlot justified by works, when she had received the messengers, and had sent them out another way?" (Jam. 2:21,25). When the Rapture happens, there will be many people still sitting in the pews, wondering why they were not taken. "Not every one that saith unto me, Lord, Lord, shall enter into the kingdom of heaven; but he that doeth the will of my Father which is in heaven" (Matt. 7:21).

It is past the hour for us to stop playing church. If you have not already done so, now is the time to bend your knee before the Father and confess you are a sinner in need of a Savior, and ask Jesus to come into your heart and be the Lord and Master of your life. And if you ask Him with a sincere heart, you *will* begin to experience change, and you *will* bring forth fruit in keeping with repentance as a natural outpouring of your love and devotion to the Lord for what He has done for you. Do not be deceived into believing you are saved if you are not. Clearly, "faith without works is dead" (Jam. 2:26).

When Jesus comes to receive the true Church unto Himself, the bodies of all believers who have died since the Day of Pentecost nearly two thousand years ago will come forth from their graves and ascend to meet Jesus in the clouds where they will join with their spirits which come with Him from heaven. "For if we believe that Jesus died and rose again, even so them also which sleep in Jesus will God bring with him" (1 Thess. 4:14). The term "fallen asleep" means believers who have died.

The ascension of the Church to meet Jesus in the clouds is called the Rapture, although nowhere in Scripture is it referred to by this title. When the Rapture occurs, Jesus will only come as far as the clouds, at which point, "the Lord himself shall descend from heaven with a shout, with the voice of the archangel, and with the trump of God: and the dead in Christ shall rise first: Then we which are alive and remain shall be caught up together with them in the clouds, to meet the Lord in the air: and so shall we ever be with the Lord" (1 Thess. 4:16–17). In this passage, the Greek translation of the phrase "shall be caught up" is the word *harpazo*, meaning "catch away." *Harpazo* is derived from the Greek word *haireomai*, meaning "to take for oneself." In the fifth century, a Latin translation of the Greek phrase "caught up" was *rapere*, and this translation formed the basis for our modern word "rapture." It involves *only* the Church-age saints, that is, all genuine believers who have placed their trust in the Lord Jesus from the Day of Pentecost forward to the Rapture.

In the parable of the rich man and Lazarus, Jesus revealed that when a believer dies, his spirit is carried away by angels to heaven (Luke 16:22). As well, Paul wrote, "to be absent from the body, and to be present with the Lord" (2 Cor. 5:8). Although at death our bodies are left to undergo decay, they will someday be resurrected to join with our spirits. For believers, there are different resurrection programs, which will be discussed in chronological order of Tribulation events. For the unbelieving dead, their spirits descend into Hades, or hell, where they will remain until their bodies are resurrected at the Great White Throne Judgment, which will occur at the conclusion of the Millennium.

Immediately after the dead in Christ rise to meet the Lord in the air, all believers who are *alive* at that time will instantly be transformed into a glorified state and also ascend to meet them in the clouds. "Behold, I shew you a mystery; We shall not all sleep, but we shall all be changed, In a moment, in the twinkling of an eye, at the last trump: for the trumpet shall sound, and the dead shall be raised incorruptible, and we shall be changed" (1 Cor. 15:51–52). But believers who are living "shall not prevent them which are asleep" (1 Thess. 4:15).

After Christ's resurrection, He appeared to His disciples over a period of forty days (Acts 1:3). When He appeared to them, they could touch Him and feel His flesh, yet He could also walk through walls. Thomas, one of the disciples, was having difficulty believing Jesus was alive. He said to the other disciples, "Except I shall see in his hands the print of the nails, and put my finger into the print of the nails, and thrust my hand into his side, I will not believe" (John 20:25). But eight days after making that statement, Scripture says, "then came Jesus, the doors being shut, and stood in the midst" (John 20:26). He turned to Thomas and said, "Reach hither thy finger, and behold my hands; and reach hither thy hand, and thrust it into my side: and be not faithless, but believing" (John 20:27). Jesus was in a glorified state, the same condition into which believers will be changed "in the twinkling of an eye."

The Church is promised deliverance from the Tribulation. Throughout Scripture, God always removed the righteous before pouring out His wrath and judgment on the unrighteous. In the case of Noah, "GOD saw that the wickedness of man was great in the earth, and that every imagination of the thoughts of his heart was only evil continually. And it repented the LORD that he had made man on the earth, and it grieved him at his heart. . . . But Noah found grace in the eyes of the LORD" (Gen. 6:5–6,8). So God destroyed the earth and all its inhabitants with a flood, but removed Noah and his family from His wrath.

Again, in the case of righteous Lot, when two angels came to visit him in the city of Sodom, the men of the city came to his door and asked him to bring the angels out in order to have homosexual relations with them. Lot pleaded with the men to take his daughters instead, but they rushed him and were about to break in the door to get to them when the angels reached out and grabbed Lot, pulling him inside. The angels then told Lot to take his family and leave the city, that the Lord was going to destroy the cities of the valley "because the cry of them is waxen great before the face of the LORD." But Lot hesitated, so the angels took him, his wife, and their two daughters and *physically* removed them from the city, and God "rained upon Sodom and upon Gomorrah brimstone and fire" (see Gen. 19:1–29). Today, all that remains of the cities are high concentrations of salt where once they stood.

It is not God's plan to put his righteous children through the Tribulation. While some may argue against the righteousness of the Church, it is true the believer's "righteousnesses are as filthy rags" (Isa. 64:6), but when we receive Jesus into our hearts as Lord and Savior, we receive an imputed righteousness through Him so that when God looks at us, He does not see the person we are, but rather, the Person of Jesus Christ, whose shed blood covers our sins. As such, "being now justified by his blood, we shall be saved from wrath through him" (Rom. 5:9).

In Revelation chapters one through three, John is on earth viewing events around him from ground level. In chapter four he, as is the Church at the Rapture, is caught up to heaven where he is viewing earth's Tribulation from above. As such, his removal before events of the Tribulation are revealed to him, depicts the Church's removal before the Tribulation begins. Clearly, the purpose of the Tribulation is not to pour out wrath upon God's beloved children. Jesus has already taken God's wrath for us at the cross. Jesus promised, "Because thou hast kept the word of my patience, I also will keep thee from the hour of temptation, which shall come upon all the world, to try them that dwell upon the earth" (Rev. 3:10).

Again, the apostle Paul urged us "to wait for his Son from heaven . . . which delivered us from the wrath to come" and that "God hath not appointed us to wrath, but to obtain salvation by our Lord Jesus Christ" (1 Thess. 1:10; 5:9).

The Rapture is designed to remove the Church to heaven while God purges sin from the earth during the remaining seven years that follow. Jesus will then return to earth at the Second Advent, occurring at the conclusion of the seven-year Tribulation, to establish His righteous thousand-year kingdom on earth. So sin must be reckoned with by the commencement of the Millennium. The Rapture and the Second Advent are two different events. This will become clearer as we progress.

There is no prophecy remaining to be fulfilled regarding the Rapture. It can happen at any moment, day or night. Paul encouraged the Church to keep "looking for that blessed hope, and the glorious appearing of the great God and our Saviour Jesus Christ" (Titus 2:13).

What Happens to the Church After the Rapture?

Judgment Seat of Christ
Scripture says, "For we must all appear before the judgment seat of Christ; that every one may receive the things done in his body, according to that he hath done, whether it be good or bad" (2 Cor. 5:10). At the Rapture, the Church is removed to heaven where we will stand before the Judgment Seat of Christ to receive our rewards for faithful service while on earth. This will occur for three and one-half years and parallel the first half of the Tribulation occurring on earth.

Believers do not face judgment for sins committed during their lifetime. Our sins are completely forgiven at the very moment we receive Jesus as our Savior, including those we will commit after receiving Him. When He died on the cross,

He paid the price for sin once and for all, and trusting in Him totally wipes our sin away, those committed in the past, the present, or those we will commit in the future. When we stand before Him at the Judgment Seat, it is solely to receive our rewards for service. "Wherefore we labour, that, whether present or absent, we may be accepted of him" (2 Cor. 5:9).

Jesus laid the foundation for how we are to live, and after salvation, believers become "labourers together with God" in the kingdom (1 Cor. 3:9). As such, "every man shall receive his own reward according to his own labour" (1 Cor. 3:8). When we stand before the Judgment Seat, our works will be thrown into fire, "and the fire shall try every man's work of what sort it is" (1 Cor. 3:13). If the work does not burn up, we will receive a reward. But "if any man's work shall be burned, he shall suffer loss: but he himself shall be saved" (1 Cor. 3:15). How many of us will "suffer loss" before the Lord on that day?

> *. . . I will give unto every one of you according to your works.*
>
> **—Revelation 2:23**

Marriage Supper of the Lamb

After receiving rewards for faithful servitude, the Church will then lay them at Jesus' feet and begin to celebrate the Marriage Supper of the Lamb in heaven for three and one-half more years, which will parallel the Great Tribulation occurring on earth. The Church is depicted in Scripture as the Bride and Jesus, the Bridegroom. After the Judgment Seat, the Bridegroom will take His Bride unto Himself and consummate the relationship, that we may be united with Him eternally. When a man and woman are joined together in marriage, there is joy at the union of the two. Scripture says,

"Husbands, love your wives, even as Christ also loved the church, and gave himself for it; That he might sanctify and cleanse it with the washing of water by the word, That he might present it to himself a glorious church, not having spot, or wrinkle, or any such thing; but that it should be holy and without blemish" (Eph. 5:25–27).

When Jesus unites with His beloved Bride in marriage, the two will experience pure, unspeakable joy unlike any wedding night on this side of heaven and one which cannot be fully appreciated until that long-awaited day.

> . . . *Blessed are they which are called unto the marriage supper of the Lamb.* . . .
>
> **—Revelation 19:9**

Chapter 5

The Players—
Who's Who in the Tribulation

A T THE COMMENCEMENT of the Tribulation, the unveiling of prophecy will rapidly begin. There are a number of key figures and terms which must be identified before we can begin the chronology. Each of these persons or celestial beings will be characterized by who they are, what their role is, when they will appear, and for how long. It is important to keep in mind, while other events are taking place, these figures will fulfill their prophetical positions simultaneously.

The Holy Spirit

The Holy Spirit is God Himself living on the inside of us (John 14:16–17; 14:20; Rom. 8:1). For believers today, the work of the Spirit is to guide and lead us into the way of truth. He reproves and convicts of sin, and also helps us in our weaknesses, interceding on our behalf to the Father with groanings too deep for words (Rom. 8:26). He illuminates the Scriptures and calls to mind the things of Jesus (John 14:26). He is our Helper, our Teacher, our Comforter, our Counselor, our Guide. But after the Rapture, His role will revert back to the days of the Old Testament.

As the third Person of the Holy Trinity, He is omniscient and omnipresent and will remain on the earth during the Tribulation. His position, however, will not be one of an indwelling ministry. To indwell believers would necessarily mean they are sealed, just as believers today are "sealed with that holy Spirit of promise" (Eph. 1:13) at the moment we receive Jesus as our Savior. But clearly, the 144,000 Jews who receive Jesus at the *beginning* of the Tribulation are sealed with the "seal of the living God" at the *midpoint*. These individuals are the only ones sealed during the Tribulation, though Scripture says "a great multitude, which no man could number, of all nations, and kindreds, and people, and tongues" (Rev. 7:9) will also receive salvation, for they are pictured standing "before the throne" of God (Rev. 7:15), wearing white robes that were washed in the blood of the Lamb. These martyred saints are not *sealed* by the Holy Spirit.

J. Dwight Pentecost put it this way:

> Apart from the indwelling ministry, Old Testament saints were said to be saved by the Holy Spirit, even though He did not indwell that believer as a temple. So in the Tribulation, the Holy Spirit will do the work of regeneration as He did when God was previously dealing with Israel, but without an indwelling ministry. The present-day indwelling is related to empowerment, to union of believer with believer because of their relationship to the Temple of God, but the indwelling is entirely distinct and separate from the work of the Spirit in regeneration.[1]

Therefore, the work of the Spirit during the Tribulation will solely be one of a regenerative nature. He will work to bring people to salvation, though not indwelling them. Just as salvation today is by faith, so will it be then, but prior to the Tribulation, believers have the indwelling Spirit "which is the earnest of our inheritance" (Eph. 1:14), thereafter guiding and enabling us to live victoriously over sin.

The Satanic Trinity
In the book of Revelation, we see the personages of the sa-

tanic trinity. In chapter twelve, Satan is depicted as the great red dragon and leader of the counterfeit trinity. In chapter thirteen, two beasts are depicted, one rising out of the sea; the other, a beast rising out of the earth. These beasts are the Antichrist and the False Prophet respectively.

In the counterfeit satanic trinity, Satan will attempt to emulate God; the Antichrist will attempt to emulate Jesus by fulfilling a covenant, albeit a false one, regarding the peaceful occupation of Israel in their land; and the False Prophet will attempt to mirror the work of the Holy Spirit by pointing men to the Antichrist as God. Satan never creates; he only counterfeits and imitates.

Satan

There are many titles given to this wicked fallen angel. He is the chief adversary of God and man, and his only purpose is to thwart God's divine plan of grace through a facade of deception. He is a destroyer, a liar, referred to by Jesus as "the wicked one" (Matt. 13:19,38). The apostle Peter even warned believers to "be sober, be vigilant; because your adversary the devil, as a roaring lion, walketh about, seeking whom he may devour" (1 Pet. 5:8).

Among Satan's many titles, the term "dragon" is most used in the book of Revelation in reference to him. "And the great dragon was cast out, that old serpent, called the Devil, and Satan" (Rev. 12:9). The "dragon" terminology was used in the Old Testament to refer to those who persecuted the children of Israel. Pharaoh is referred to as "the great dragon." Scripture says, "Behold, I am against thee, Pharaoh king of Egypt, the great dragon that lieth in the midst of his rivers" (Ezek. 29:3). As well, Nebuchadnezzar is likened to a "dragon" for his persecution of Israel. "Nebuchadrezzar the king of Babylon hath devoured me, . . . he hath swallowed me up like a dragon" (Jer. 51:34). And so it is today. Persecution is a way of life for every child of God, and the more we try to live godly, the more persecution we face. The apostle Paul wrote, "Yea, and all that will live godly in Christ Jesus shall suffer persecution" (2 Tim. 3:12).

Satan is the ruler of this world. He is the cause of sin and rebellion. Jesus Himself referred to Satan three times as the "prince of the world," while Paul referred to him as the "god of this world." Satan will control the activity of the counterfeit trinity throughout the Tribulation, but he will physically indwell the body of the Antichrist at the midpoint.

The Antichrist

In the Scriptures, there are approximately thirty titles given to the Antichrist. The name Antichrist is derived from the word "anti," meaning "against," coupled with his activity in the satanic trinity paralleling that of Christ's in the Godhead. During the Tribulation, he will be "anti-Christ," emulating a Christ-like persona of peace, yet completely against God and His Son.

Among his many titles, he is referred to as the beast, the wicked one, the violent man, the Assyrian, the spoiler, the little horn, the willful king, the man of sin, the son of perdition, the lawless one, the desolator, and the head of many countries, to name a few.

The prophet Daniel recorded in detail events surrounding the "time of the end" when the Antichrist would emerge. These will be revealed as we progress chronologically. He also recorded specific information regarding the Antichrist himself. Daniel described him as large in appearance, having a fierce countenance (Dan. 7:20; 8:23). He will be skilled in speech and powerful, though not by his own power (Dan. 8:23–24). He will speak blasphemous words against Almighty God, having no regard for Him or the desire of women (Rev. 13:5; Dan. 11:36–37). He will perform signs and false wonders (2 Thess. 2:9).

The Antichrist will not appear until the Church is Raptured. At the beginning of the Tribulation, he will emerge out of a ten-nation European alliance and bring peace to Israel. He will be extremely well-liked by all the nations and ultimately elevated to world ruler by the midpoint of the Tribulation, possessing "power . . . over all kindreds, and tongues, and nations" (Rev. 13:7). Scripture says, "And all that dwell upon the earth shall worship him, whose names are not written in the book of life of the Lamb slain from the foundation of the world" (Rev. 13:8). He will rule the world for three and one-half years, from the second half of the Tribulation onward. "Power was given unto him to continue forty and two months" (Rev. 13:5; see also Rev. 12:14).

Though the Antichrist emerges at the beginning of the Tribulation, his true evil persona will not be manifested until Satan physically indwells his body at the midpoint and onward to its end. Throughout the Tribulation, however, the Antichrist will be the key figure in the satanic trinity. He will be guided by Satan during the first half and possessed by him in the second. When the devil indwells the Antichrist, the Great Tribulation will begin—the "time of Jacob's trouble." It will be a time of distress "such as never was since there was a nation even to that same time" (Dan. 12:1). Scripture warns, "Woe to the inhabiters of the earth and of the sea! for the devil is come down unto you, having great wrath, because he knoweth that he hath but a short time" (Rev. 12:12). At that point, the Antichrist will begin his slaughter of the Jews and of those who accept Jesus as Lord after the Rapture.

Contrary to popular belief, the Antichrist will be a nonobservant Jew. In Revelation 7, a divine seal is placed on the foreheads of 144,000 Jews, twelve thousand from each of the twelve tribes of Israel. This takes place at the midpoint of the Tribulation to protect them from the Antichrist's persecution during the latter half. However, the tribe of Dan is omitted. They are not sealed and will not be protected by God. While no one knows for sure why this is so, a popular belief is because of their many idolatrous acts throughout Jewish history. But a better explanation may be found in the Antichrist being a descendant from this tribe. God will not protect the tribe of Dan because one of their members will be possessed by Satan, who will slaughter millions of Jews.

Scripture says, "Dan shall be a serpent by the way, an adder in the path" (Gen. 49:17). Since the Antichrist will likely come from the tribe of Dan, the characterization of Dan as a "serpent" may be seen in the Antichrist's federation with Satan, who is referred to as the serpent. In this same passage, the Bible refers to an adder. This serpent is a venomous viper found in the region of the Near East, or Europe, where the Antichrist will emerge. And Daniel used a like description in referring to the Antichrist as "the little horn."

Another reason why we believe him to be a Jew is because Daniel recorded, "Neither shall he regard the God of his fathers" (Dan. 11:37). The phrase "God of his fathers" is a common phrase used no less than forty-eight times in the Scriptures by the Jews when referring to God. In other words, the Jewish Antichrist will have no regard for his God.

Finally, while most of the Jews still await their Messiah, when a man emerges with miraculous powers, bringing peace to Israel, and a religious figure who also performs many miracles proclaims the man of peace to actually be God, the Jews will be convinced he is their long-awaited Messiah. They would not accept him as such if he were not a Jew. Jesus said, "I am come in my Father's name, and ye receive me not: if another shall come in his own name, him ye will receive" (John 5:43).

Parenthetically, when the Jews were dispersed in the Diaspora, the descendants of the tribe of Dan migrated in a northwesterly direction, mainly into the Balkan area. As they settled, to remain true to their heritage, they named many locations after their ancestral father, Dan, oftentimes using his name as a root form. For example, there is the Danube River, which runs through the Balkan states. They also retained the name throughout their ancestry, much as we do today in naming our children after a parent or grandparent. It is interesting to note the key writer on the Antichrist is Daniel, whose ancestry is unidentified. This in no way implies Daniel was evil; in fact, we know that he was exceedingly godly. But by Daniel writing about the Antichrist, who will come from the tribe of Dan, we see the mystery and magnificence of God, who reveals truth to the honest seeker, and we know there are no coincidences with Him.

The Antichrist will emerge at the onset of the Tribulation and remain until Jesus returns to earth at the end of the Tribulation. Though Scripture says the beast will suffer a fatal head wound and his head is then healed (Rev. 13:3,12,14), this is symbolic of the revived Roman Empire and should not be misinterpreted as a resurrection of the Antichrist. The beast is seen coming out of the sea, having seven heads and ten horns (Rev. 13:1). One of the seven heads suffers a fatal wound, but later we see that the seven heads are seven kings (Rev. 17:10). Therefore, a more likely explanation is that the seven heads depict the seven world empires in the Bible, to include Egypt, Assyria, Babylon, Medo-Persia, Greece, and Rome. The head which suffers a mortal wound and then comes to life depicts Rome and, thereafter, the revived Roman Empire. Finally, Satan has no power to give life, and try as he might, he cannot resurrect anyone. So if the Antichrist died, he would stay dead.

The False Prophet
Jesus said, "Then if any man shall say unto you, Lo, here is

Christ, or there; believe it not" (Matt. 24:23). Shortly before the midpoint of the Tribulation while the Antichrist is rising in power, the False Prophet will emerge. As the third component of the satanic trinity, he will attempt to emulate the ministry of the Holy Spirit in the Godhead. Just as the Holy Spirit directs believers in the worship of Jesus Christ, the False Prophet will direct the world into the worship of the Antichrist. "And he . . . causeth the earth and them which dwell therein to worship the first beast" (Rev. 13:12). Because he is depicted as a lamb, he will likely be or have been a religious figure (Rev. 13:11).

Over sixteen hundred years ago, the prophet Malachi told of the appearance of Elijah before the coming day of the Lord. Because most Jews do not believe their Messiah has come, they continue to await the arrival of Elijah to herald the approach of their Messiah. Indeed, Elijah *will* appear at the beginning of the Tribulation, but as one of the Two Witnesses of God. He will not be recognized by the Jews, for he will be a prophet of judgment, exacting punishment for three and one-half years during the first half of the Tribulation in an effort to turn men's hearts to repentance.

Knowing the Jews await the appearance of Elijah to precede Christ, the False Prophet will seize the opportunity for deception, sporting a profile of Elijah the Jews will accept. Second Kings 1:1–16 reveals the account of Elijah causing fire to rain down from heaven, consuming King Ahaziah's messengers. The king fell through lattice in his upper chamber, and as a result of his injuries, became seriously ill. As such, he sent messengers to Elijah to determine whether he would recover. But because he initially sought the advice of a foreign god, Elijah was granted authority to destroy the messengers by raining fire down from heaven and consuming them. The False Prophet will have the same power. "And he doeth great wonders, so that he maketh fire come down from heaven on the earth in the sight of men" (Rev. 13:13). The Jews are intimately familiar with Elijah's record of miracles, and as such, they will believe the False Prophet is Elijah. Because Malachi warned Elijah would precede the Lord, when the False Prophet claims the man who secured Israel's peace in his initial rise to world power is indeed their long-awaited Messiah, the Jews will believe it.

The two will exhibit miraculous power. Jesus warned of this. "For there shall arise false Christs, and false prophets, and shall shew great signs and wonders; insomuch that, if it were possible, they shall deceive the very elect" (Matt. 24:24). The False Prophet will be limited in his ability to perform miracles. His power will only operate in the presence of the Antichrist. "And deceiveth them that dwell on the earth by the means of those miracles which he had power to do in the sight of the beast" (Rev. 13:14).

The False Prophet will administer the worldwide Mark of the Beast system beginning at the midpoint of the Tribulation. "And he causeth all, both small and great, rich and poor, free and bond, to receive a mark in their right hand, or in their foreheads: And that no man might buy or sell, save he that had the mark, or the name of the beast, or the number of his name" (Rev. 13:16–17).

Once the False Prophet emerges, sometime within the first half of the Tribulation, he will remain until Jesus returns to earth at the end of the Tribulation.

The 144,000 Jewish Witnesses

After the Church is removed at the Rapture, God will turn His attention to the nation of Israel. By a supernatural occurrence, 144,000 Jews scattered throughout the world will receive salvation, twelve thousand from each of the twelve tribes of Israel, except Dan (Rev. 7:1–8). In Dan's place is the tribe of Levi, who are not usually included when reference is made to the twelve tribes of Israel. They were set apart by God for priestly service, and therefore He was their inheritance (Deut. 10:9). Though the tribe of Dan will not be divinely sealed during the Tribulation, they will be restored to inhabit the northernmost region of Israel during Christ's millennial reign on earth (Ezek. 48:1).

The origin of the twelve tribes of Israel is recorded in the book of Genesis, beginning with the life of Jacob. Chapter thirty reveals the twelve sons who were born to him. Then in chapter thirty-five, God changed Jacob's name to Israel. Each of Israel's (Jacob) twelve sons became fathers, and their descendants became what is known as the twelve "tribes" of Israel, the Israelites. Each descending tribe was named after their ancestral father, one of Israel's sons.

No one knows what supernatural event will cause the 144,000 Jews to accept Jesus as their Savior, but throughout the Tribulation they will preach to the world of the coming Messiah. It appears the Spirit of God moves sovereignly to bring about their conversion. Just as the apostle Paul "saw the light" when he encountered the Lord on the road to Damascus (Acts 26), something miraculous will occur in the lives of these 144,000 Jews. Paul's conversion to Christ represents a prototype of what the 144,000 Jews will experience. Their ministry will be worldwide, and the effect of their message will result in "a great multitude, which no man could number" (Rev. 7:9), repenting and accepting Jesus as their Savior.

The Two Witnesses of God

At the beginning of the Tribulation, two men dressed in sackcloth will appear in Israel, preaching judgment and repentance, for the coming of the Lord is at hand. Sackcloth is a black garment made of angora goat hair, usually worn over another garment as a symbol of judgment. It was worn during Old Testament days by mourners and prophets.

Speculation abounds as to the identity of these two men. Some believe them to be Elijah and Moses; others believe them to be Elijah and Enoch; while still others believe them to be only spiritual representations of the Old Testament prophets.

However, regarding the identity of the first witness, Jesus said, "Elias truly shall first come, and restore all things" (Matt. 17:11). As well, the prophet Malachi foretold the appearance of Elijah before the Lord returns. "Behold, I will send my messenger, and he shall prepare the way before me" (Mal. 3:1). This is not to be confused with John the Baptist, because the following verse says, "But who may abide the day of his coming? and who shall stand when he appeareth?" (Mal. 3:2). This is an obvious reference to the time preceding Christ's second coming to earth. Malachi then clears up any confusion as to the timing of Elijah's appearance. "Behold, I will send you Elijah the prophet before the coming of the great and dreadful day of the LORD" (Mal. 4:5). And Jesus Himself confirmed, "Elias truly shall first come" (Matt. 17:11).

Elijah was the preeminent prophet of judgment. Just as Elijah prayed and stopped the rain for three and one-half years (1 Kings 17:1), the Two Witnesses will possess the same power, also stopping the rain for three and one-half years. "And I will give power unto my two witnesses, and they shall prophesy a thousand two hundred and threescore days, clothed in sackcloth. . . . These have power to shut heaven, that it rain not in the days of their prophecy" (Rev. 11:3,6).

A strong argument may also be made for Elijah's identity as one of the Two Witnesses because he did not experience physical death. He was transported into heaven in his physical body. "And it came to pass, as they still went on, and talked, that, behold, there appeared a chariot of fire, and horses of fire, and parted them both asunder; and Elijah went up by a whirlwind into heaven" (2 Kings 2:11). Because the prophet did not die, this possibly suggests God carried him to heaven to someday place him back on the earth as one of the two prophets of judgment, who will then experience death.

But most of the speculation surrounding the Two Witnesses lies in the identity of the second witness. Clearly, Elijah is the first. However, strong argument is made for both Enoch or Moses as the second witness.

Enoch, like Elijah, was a prophet of judgment. Jude referenced Enoch's prophecy regarding the return of Christ. He wrote, "Behold, the Lord cometh with ten thousands of his saints, To execute judgment upon all, and to convince all that are ungodly among them of all their ungodly deeds which they have ungodly committed, and of all their hard speeches which ungodly sinners have spoken against him" (Jude 14–15). Enoch also did not experience physical death. "And Enoch walked with God: and he was not; for God took him" (Gen. 5:24). This possibly suggests he will be the second prophet of judgment.

However, Moses was the man used by God to establish the Law for Israel. Jesus said, "Think not that I am come to destroy the law, or the prophets: I am not come to destroy, but to fulfil" (Matt. 5:17). Therefore, because the Law came through Moses, he also is a likely candidate for the second witness. As well, Moses turned water into blood and smote the land of Egypt with plagues (Exod. 7:14–21). The Two Witnesses will do the same. "These . . . have power over waters to turn them to blood, and to smite the earth with all plagues, as often as they will" (Rev. 11:6).

Finally, and perhaps the most popular reason the second witness is believed to be Moses, is he stood with Elijah and Jesus on the Mount of Transfiguration, discussing Christ's imminent death. Because of this, it is therefore held he will appear with Elijah to announce Christ's imminent return.

Whoever the Two Witnesses are, their ministry will be confined to the nation of Israel. They will appear immediately after the Rapture and remain throughout the first half of the Tribulation, preaching a message of judgment and repentance. Anyone who attempts to harm them will be killed instantly by fire, which will proceed out of their mouths. "And if any man will hurt them, fire proceedeth out of their mouth, and devoureth their enemies" (Rev. 11:5). Their ministry will last exactly twelve hundred and sixty days (Rev. 11:3), not one day more or less. When their time is complete, God will allow their deaths.

The Three Angels
During His Olivet Discourse, Jesus said, "And this gospel of the kingdom shall be preached in all the world for a witness unto all nations; and then shall the end come" (Matt. 24:14). This verse has been the catalyst for today's worldwide evangelistic revival in hopes of delaying no longer the return of Christ. While evangelizing is certainly commanded in the Great Commission (Matt. 28:19–20; Mark 16:15), the days have been allotted until the time of the end, and they will not be expedited by man's evangelizing efforts.

In fact, the final spreading of the gospel to the whole world will not be by human agency, but rather, the work of the first of three angels flying in midheaven, who will appear at the midpoint and into the second half of the Tribulation preceding Christ's return to earth. "And I saw another angel fly in the midst of heaven, having the everlasting gospel to preach unto them that dwell on the earth, and to every nation, and kindred, and tongue, and people, Saying with a loud voice, Fear God, and give glory to him; for the hour of his judgment is come: and worship him that made heaven, and earth, and the sea, and the fountains of waters" (Rev. 14:6–7).

The second angel follows behind the first, saying, "Babylon is fallen, is fallen, that great city, because she made all nations drink of the wine of the wrath of her fornication" (Rev. 14:8). This refers to the nations of the world being deceived by the false religious system, accepting the testimony of the False Prophet in worshiping the Antichrist as God.

The third angels follows behind the first two angels

> . . . saying with a loud voice, If any man worship the beast and his image, and receive his mark in his forehead, or in his hand, The same shall drink of the wine of the wrath of God, which is poured out without mixture into the cup of his indignation; and he shall be tormented with fire and brimstone in the presence of the holy angels, and in the presence of the Lamb: And the smoke of their torment ascendeth up for ever and ever: and they have no rest day nor night, who worship the beast and his image, and whosoever receiveth the mark of his name.
>
> —Revelation 14:9–11

Endnotes

1. J. Dwight Pentecost, *Things to Come* (Zondervan Publishing House, Grand Rapids, Michigan, 1958), p. 271.

Chapter 6

The Seals, Trumpets, and Bowls of Wrath

BEFORE WE CAN FULLY understand the seals, trumpets, and bowls of wrath, we must look at the scroll which the seven seals surround. It is not a coincidence that a similar scroll appears several times in the Scriptures and then appears a final time in Revelation 5 as the scroll Jesus opens to begin judgment during the Tribulation.

As we proceed with the seals, trumpets, and bowls of wrath, this chapter may seem somewhat complicated. It would be very helpful to the reader to actually refer to the Bible passages stated herein. In so doing, you will better grasp the correlations given.

The Scroll
We begin with the prophet Jeremiah. Before Jeremiah wrote his scroll, God told him:

> Thus saith the LORD; Stand in the court of the LORD's house, and speak unto all the cities of Judah, which come to worship in the LORD's house, all the words that I command thee to speak unto them; diminish not a word: If so be they will hearken, and turn every man from his evil way, that I may repent me of the evil, which I purpose to do unto them because of the evil of their doings. And thou shalt say unto

them, Thus saith the LORD; If ye will not hearken to me, to walk in my law, which I have set before you, To hearken to the words of my servants the prophets, whom I sent unto you, both rising up early, and sending them, but ye have not hearkened; Then will I make this house like Shiloh, and will make this city a curse to all the nations of the earth.

—Jeremiah 26:2–6

Jeremiah did as he was told, and afterward, the Lord instructed him again, saying

Take thee a roll of a book, and write therein all the words that I have spoken unto thee against Israel, and against Judah, and against all the nations, from the day I spake unto thee, from the days of Josiah, even unto this day. It may be that the house of Judah will hear all the evil which I purpose to do unto them; that they may return every man from his evil way; that I may forgive their iniquity and their sin.

—Jeremiah 36:2–3

Likewise, he did as the Lord instructed, and when it was all said and done, the scroll contained twenty-three years of Jeremiah's exhortation of Israel to repent or suffer complete destruction (Jer. 25). It was read aloud twice to the Jews, once in the Temple court and once before the Jewish princes. We do not know what was written on the scroll, but whatever it contained, Scripture says, "when they had heard all the words, they were afraid both one and other" (Jer. 36:16). It was then partially read to Judah's King Jehoiakim, who cut it up and burned it. Thereafter, the Lord instructed Jeremiah to rewrite the scroll verbatim (Jer. 36:28), which he did "and there were added besides unto them many like words" (Jer. 36:32). Jeremiah wept and lamented for his people, but they continued in their rebellion toward God.

The Lord then called the prophet Ezekiel to exhort the Jews to repentance, and a scroll was handed to him, which appears to be the same scroll Jeremiah rewrote after King Jehoiakim burned it, possibly including the book of Lamentations as the "many like words" he added to the scroll. The book of Lamentations was written by Jeremiah, which contains five poems of mourning for the destruction of Jerusalem. Scripture indicates the scroll handed to Ezekiel "was written within and without: and there was written therein lamentations, and mourning, and woe" (Ezek. 2:10). Indeed, their failure to heed the warnings resulted in the destruction of Jerusalem at the hands of the Babylonians in 586 B.C., then again in A.D. 70 at the hands of the Romans, and it will occur a final time during the second half of the Tribulation surrounding the "woe" trumpet judgments and bowls of wrath.

It appears this same scroll "spoken unto thee against Israel, and against Judah, and against all the nations" (Jer. 36:2) was recorded yet again in the Scriptures by the prophet Zechariah, who sees the scroll in a vision. This time it is flying unrolled in midair, measuring thirty feet long and fifteen feet wide. Zechariah is told the scroll is "the curse that goeth forth over the face of the whole earth" (Zech. 5:1–3), which coincides with Jeremiah's words in which Israel will be a "curse to all the nations of the earth" (Jer. 26:6). The prophet Isaiah also wrote, "Therefore hath the curse devoured the earth, and they that dwell therein are desolate: therefore the inhabitants of the earth are burned, and few men left" (Isa. 24:6).

Finally, in Revelation 5, we see what again appears to be the same scroll. While in exile on the tiny island of Patmos, John the apostle was given the vision of end-time events as revealed in the book of Revelation. In ancient days, scrolls were customarily written on one side only, yet the scroll handed to Ezekiel, the flying scroll Zechariah saw, and the scroll in Revelation 5 were all written on the front and back, except the scroll in Revelation 5 now has seven seals around it.

Archaeologists have discovered thousands of seals dating back four thousand years before Christ. A seal was a specially crafted device characterized by an insignia, usually made of metal or precious stones and shaped into finger rings. When an item was to be sealed, soft clay or melted wax would be placed on the item. The seal was then pressed into the clay or wax, bearing its insignia. Among their several uses, seals were placed over important books and documents which were to remain closed.

The Lord knew Israel would not repent at the exhortations of Jeremiah and Ezekiel, so following their respective ministries, he used another man to reveal Israel's ultimate fate. While in Babylonian captivity, a panoramic future of the Jewish nation was revealed to Daniel by the angel Gabriel (Dan. 9:24–26). Later, Daniel saw a terrifying vision of great conflict and was told the vision pertains to the Jews in the latter days (Dan. 10:1,14). A lengthy explanation was given to Daniel concerning Israel's great conflict, and afterward, he was instructed to "shut up the words, and seal the book, even to the time of the end" (Dan. 12:4). However, it was not the words in the book of Daniel that were to be sealed, but rather, the *vision* Daniel saw regarding Israel in the latter days. Isaiah had a similar experience with his prophetical end-time visions. Scripture says, "And the vision of all is become unto you as the words of a book that is sealed" (Isa. 29:11), or *ciphrah* in the Hebrew, meaning scroll. When Daniel asked, "What shall be the end of these things?" the angel responded, "Go thy way, Daniel: for the words are closed up and sealed till the time of the end" (Dan. 12:8–9).

Therefore, with the original scroll written by Jeremiah regarding the fate of Israel and the world for failing to repent, which was then handed to Ezekiel to proclaim the same message, along with Zechariah's vision of the scroll being a curse going forth over the whole earth, all these descriptions of the scroll combined with Daniel's vision of Israel's future instructed to be sealed up until the end of time, it appears events in his panoramic vision of Israel *are* the seven seals around the scroll depicting the events of the Tribulation regarding Israel's great conflict, which will also involve all the nations of the world. It is important to remember that with the removal of the Church at the Rapture, God will redirect His attention to Israel for the remaining seven years, and *they* are the focus of the Tribulation.

In Revelation 5, God is sitting on His throne holding the scroll in His right hand. The Lord Jesus then comes forth to take the scroll from God, and He begins to break it open, one seal at a time.

The Seals: Four Horsemen of the Apocalypse

Perhaps one of the most common misunderstandings of the seven-year Tribulation is that of the seal, trumpet, and bowl judgments. There are seven components of each judgment, that is, seven seals, seven trumpets, and seven bowls of wrath. However, contrary to popular belief, they do not happen in succession, but rather, they overlap and coincide throughout the Tribulation. For example, the seal judgments provide an *overview* of the *entire* Tribulation period, with the trumpet and bowl judgments depicted within the seals. As well, the last three trumpets coincide with the bowls of wrath during the Great Tribulation, or the second three and one-half years. As I explain the seals, trumpets, and bowls, I will establish their point of origin in the Tribulation.

Six of the seven seal judgments are recorded in Revelation 6. As stated, the seals are an overview of the entire Tribulation. The first four seals reveal the Four Horsemen of the Apocalypse. As riders, they are symbolic of what is to transpire on the earth, again bearing in mind that Israel is the focus of the Tribulation.

John writes of the first horseman, "And I saw, and behold a white horse: and he that sat on him had a bow; and a crown was given unto him: and he went forth conquering, and to conquer" (Rev. 6:2). It has long been held the first horseman depicts the Antichrist because he is seen riding a white horse, which symbolizes peace, while wearing a crown and carrying a bow with no arrows, indicating his false agenda. He is also seen going forth to conquer. There are others who believe the first horseman depicts Jesus Himself *because* of the white horse and crown the rider is given. However, the First Horseman of the Apocalypse may well represent, instead, the 144,000 Jews who evangelize throughout the Tribulation period.

When we take a closer look at this passage, we see a parallel to the white horse found in Revelation 19. In this passage, the riders on white horses are the Lord Jesus and the raptured saints returning to the battle of Armageddon (Rev. 19:11,14). Though they return to battle, none of the saints possess any weapons of warfare, indicating the victory has already been won at the cross. When the 144,000 Jews begin evangelizing at the beginning of the Tribulation, they are seen carrying a bow with no arrows because they are going forth with the Word of God, which *is* their weapon of warfare. The psalmist wrote, "If he turn not, he will whet his sword; he hath bent his bow, and made it ready" (Ps. 7:12). And the apostle Paul tells us, "the sword of the Spirit . . . is the word of God" (Eph. 6:17).

The fact that the first horseman has a bow with no arrows cannot in and of itself link this rider to the Antichrist because there are thirty-seven other references in Scripture to bows with no arrows, and in five passages, God Himself provides an arrow. "When I have bent Judah for me, filled the bow with Ephraim, . . . the LORD shall be seen over them, and his arrow shall go forth as the lightning" (Zech. 9:13–14). And, "God shall shoot at them with an arrow" (Ps. 64:7). Therefore, a more likely explanation for the bow with no arrows may be the Word of God and the message of salvation going forth from the 144,000 Jews.

Also, the first horseman is seen wearing a crown. Upon salvation, believers are given a crown. Once the 144,000 Jews are converted, they too will receive a crown. Jesus said, "Behold, I come quickly: hold that fast which thou hast, that no man take thy crown" (Rev. 3:11).

Finally, we see the first horseman going forth "conquering, and to conquer." The definition for "conquer" means "to overcome." At the beginning of the Tribulation, the 144,000 Jewish witnesses will preach to the world of its need for salvation and the coming of Christ. *They* are the ones who will go forth "conquering, and to conquer," and those who receive salvation are the ones who overcome the perils of the Tribulation by holding on to their faith. Scripture says, "For whatsoever is born of God overcometh the world: and this is the victory that overcometh the world, even our faith" (1 John 5:4). The only other reference, or any derivation thereof, to the word "conquer" in the King James Version of the Bible is found in Romans 8:37, where it says believers overwhelmingly conquer "through him that loved us"

Therefore, the first seal, being the First Horseman of the Apocalypse, likely depicts the 144,000 Jewish evangelists. This seal, and the message of the gospel, will span the entirety of the Tribulation. Ultimately these Jews will enter into the Millennium in their physical bodies, having been instrumental in bringing "a great multitude, which no man could number, of all nations, and kindreds, and people, and tongues" (Rev. 7:9) to salvation.

The Second Horseman of the Apocalypse is granted "to take peace from the earth, and that they should kill one another: and there was given unto him a great sword" (Rev. 6:3–4). The red color of this horse depicts bloodshed. While some believe this seal represents war, it more likely refers to the Antichrist's worldwide persecution of the Jews and believers throughout the second half of the Tribulation. During the first half, there will be a false peace on earth, but with the second horseman, peace will be removed at the midpoint when the Antichrist betrays Israel. At that point, men will indeed slay one another, just as the second seal depicts. Jesus warned, "the time cometh, that whosoever killeth you will think that he doeth God service" (John 16:2). He said, "And the brother shall deliver up the brother to death, and the father the child: and the children shall rise up against their parents, and cause them to be put to death." He added, "Think not that I am come to send peace on earth: I came not to send peace, but a sword" (Matt. 10:21,34), in fact, a "great sword," as is given the second horseman. This second seal is placed in time beginning at the midpoint of the Tribulation and continuing throughout the second half, overlapping the "woe" trumpet judgments and the bowls of wrath.

The Third Horseman of the Apocalypse produces famine (Rev. 6:5–6). The black color of this horse depicts disease and resultant death. This seal obviously coincides with the ministry of the Two Witness of God in Israel during the first half of the Tribulation. They are given the power "to shut heaven, that it rain not in the days of their prophecy . . . and to smite the earth with all plagues, as often as they will" (Rev. 11:6). Ezekiel recorded that a third of Israel will die by plague or be consumed by famine (Ezek. 5:12). The ministry of the Two Witnesses will last exactly twelve hundred sixty days, until the midpoint of the Tribulation.

The Fourth Horseman of the Apocalypse brings forth death (Rev. 6:7–8). His horse is pale in color. The Greek word for "pale" is *chloros*, meaning a sickly yellowish-green color. From *chloros*, the English word "chlorine" is derived. In fact, chlorine is a heavy yellow-green gas. This seal likely depicts the War of Gog and Magog, which will occur shortly before the midpoint of the Tribulation. The prophet Ezekiel warned of this war nearly twenty-six hundred years ago (Ezek. 38–39). As the seals provide an overview of the entire Tribulation, the destruction of a third of the earth as revealed in the first four trumpets (Rev. 8:6–12) coincide with the devastation of the fourth seal. Chemical warfare will be a likely component of this war, which may explain the pale-colored horse.

In this fourth seal judgment, this rider is called Death; and Hades follows him. "And power was given unto them over the fourth part of the earth, to kill with sword, and with hunger, and with death, and with the beasts of the earth" (Rev. 6:8). When we look at the War of Gog and Magog in Ezekiel, we see the same perilous conditions. God said, "Every man's sword shall be against his brother. And I will plead against him with pestilence and with blood; . . . I will give thee unto the ravenous birds of every sort, and to the beasts of the field to be devoured" (Ezek. 38:21–22; 39:4). Again, this seal coincides with the first four trumpet judgments of Revelation 8, beginning shortly before the midpoint of the Tribulation.

The fifth seal depicts the Tribulation martyrs (Rev. 6:9–11). They are dressed in white robes (vs. 11) and pictured underneath the altar in heaven, having been "slain for the word of God, and for the testimony which they held" (Rev. 6:9). The persecution of believers does not take place until the second half of the Tribulation. "These which are arrayed in white robes . . . are they which came out of great tribulation" (Rev. 7:13–14). Therefore, this seal overlaps in time with the conditions surrounding the "woe" trumpet judgments and the bowls of wrath.

The sixth seal depicts the campaign of Armageddon (Rev.

6:12–17), and coincides with the last three trumpets and the seven bowls of wrath, which all relate to Armageddon (Rev. 9, 16). This seal warns of a "great earthquake" in which "every mountain and island were moved out of their places" (Rev. 6:14). Likewise, the seventh bowl of wrath warns of a "great earthquake" where "every island fled away, and the mountains were not found" (Rev. 16:18,20).

In the sixth seal, "the heaven departed as a scroll when it is rolled together" (Rev. 6:14). Isaiah used the same description in reference to Armageddon when all the armies of the world converge on Israel. He writes, "For the indignation of the LORD is upon all nations, and his fury upon all their armies: he hath utterly destroyed them. . . . The mountains shall be melted with their blood. And all the host of heaven shall be dissolved, and the heavens shall be rolled together as a scroll" (Isa. 34:2–4).

John says in the sixth seal, "the sun became black as sackcloth of hair, and the moon became as blood" (Rev. 6:12). The prophet Joel recorded the same scene before Jesus returns to earth at the battle of Armageddon. He wrote, "And I will shew wonders in the heavens and in the earth, blood, and fire, and pillars of smoke. The sun shall be turned into darkness, and the moon into blood, before the great and the terrible day of the LORD come" (Joel 2:30–31).

Finally, the sixth seal describes the kings of the earth hiding themselves in caves, crying out to the mountains to fall on them and to hide them "from the face of him that sitteth on the throne, and from the wrath of the Lamb: For the great day of his wrath is come; and who shall be able to stand?" (Rev. 6:16–17). This coincides with the seventh trumpet, where the temple of God in heaven is opened up. These men actually see God in the sky seated on His throne (Rev. 11:19), which is why they are seen running and hiding. At that point, Jesus returns in wrath to slay them (Rev. 11:18; 19:21). I believe the sky opening up to reveal God in His temple is the sign Jesus spoke of that would appear in the sky before He returned to earth (Matt. 24:30).

Therefore, this sixth seal is placed in time at the conclusion of the Tribulation and coincides with the campaign of Armageddon as revealed in the last three trumpets and all seven bowls of wrath.

The seventh and final seal produces the seven trumpet judgments (Rev. 8).

The Trumpets

The trumpet judgments are recorded in Revelation 8, 9, and 11:15–19. As mentioned, they are incorporated within the seal judgments, but they provide more insight into the devastating conditions on earth during the Tribulation. The first four begin just prior to the midpoint, while the last three span the second half and are commonly referred to as the "woe" judgments. The trumpets are symbolic and characterize the ravages of warfare. Bear in mind the prophetical writers could only describe what they saw to the best of their ability, while we have the benefit of understanding their visions based on the development of weapons which match their description.

At the sounding of the first trumpet, a third of the earth, a third of the trees, and all the green grass is burned up. At the second trumpet, "a great mountain burning with fire was cast into the sea" (Rev. 8:8), and a third of the sea turns to blood, killing a third of the creatures in the sea and also destroying a third of the ships. Notice the reference to "sea" and not "seas," plural. This likely represents the Mediterranean Sea, the sea of the Bible. At the third trumpet, a great star called "Wormwood" is seen falling from heaven, burning "as it were a lamp." It falls on the rivers and springs of waters, making them bitter. At the fourth trumpet, a third of the sun, moon, and stars are darkened.

These first four trumpets are placed in time just shortly before the midpoint of the Tribulation and befit the carnage described in Ezekiel 38 and 39 surrounding the War of Gog and Magog. The fourth seal judgment and the first four trumpets coincide with each other.

Recalling the fourth seal, authority is given to kill over a fourth of the earth's population, yet with the first four trumpets, a third of the earth is destroyed. The War of Gog and Magog will involve a number of Middle Eastern Arab nations, Israel, Russia, Eastern Europe, and several countries in northern Africa. When we look at a world map, this region clearly comprises a third of the earth. Likewise, this densely population region could account for a quarter of the world's population, or 1.5 billion people.

The remaining three trumpets are referred to as the "woe" judgments because of the eagle which flies in midheaven, saying, "Woe, woe, woe, to the inhabiters of the earth by reason of the other voices of the trumpet of the three angels, which are yet to sound!" (Rev. 8:13). They begin at the midpoint, commencing the Great Tribulation. Jesus warned, "For then shall be great tribulation, such as was not since the beginning of the world to this time, no, nor ever shall be. And except those days should be shortened, there should no flesh be saved: but for the elect's sake those days shall be shortened" (Matt. 24:21–22).

The fifth and sixth trumpets are incorporated within the sixth seal and also parallel the seven bowls of wrath. They depict horrors beginning at the midpoint and into the second half of the Tribulation, the Great Tribulation. When Satan indwells the body of the Antichrist at the midpoint of the Tribulation, he begins his worldwide slaughter. Scripture says, "Woe to the inhabiters of the earth and of the sea! for the devil is come down unto you, having great wrath, because he knoweth that he hath but a short time" (Rev. 12:12). At that point, only twelve hundred sixty days remain in the Tribulation. Satan hates God and all who belong to Him, and for the remaining three and one-half years, he unleashes his fury on God's beloved children. "And when the dragon [Satan] saw that he was cast unto the earth, he persecuted the woman [Israel] which brought forth the man child. . . . And the dragon was wroth with the woman, and went to make war with the remnant of her seed, which keep the commandments of God, and have the testimony of Jesus Christ" (Rev. 12:13,17).

With the sounding of the fifth trumpet, the first of three "woe" judgments, Satan will physically possess the body of the Antichrist for the remainder of the Tribulation. As such, he is the preeminent force in bringing complete and total world chaos. He immediately opens the pit of hell and locusts are unleashed on the earth. They are not permitted to "kill them, but that they should be tormented five months: and their torment was as the torment of a scorpion, when he striketh a man" (Rev. 9:5). The pain and anguish inflicted by this judgment will cause men to seek death. They will long to die, but death will flee from them (Rev. 9:6).

These locusts may truly be demonic in nature or they may be symbolic of troops in warfare. We find a parallel account of locusts recorded in the book of Joel. The prophet saw a vision of various types of locusts which would someday devastate the land of Israel. In Joel's vision, the locusts are identified as "nation . . . strong, and without number" (Joel 1:6). Regarding this invading force, he wrote, "A day of darkness and of gloominess, a day of clouds and of thick darkness, as the morning spread upon the mountains: a great people and a strong; there hath not been ever the like, neither shall be any more after it" (Joel 2:2). The locusts are also identified by God as "my great army" (Joel 2:25).

Additionally, when we compare the appearance of Joel's locusts to those in Revelation, they match indentically. Both have teeth as the teeth of lions (Joel 1:6; Rev. 9:8), both make noise as the sound of many chariots (Joel 2:5; Rev. 9:9), both have the appearance of horses running to battle (Joel 2:4; Rev. 9:7,9), and the locusts in Revelation have faces like "the faces of men" (Rev. 9:7), matching Joel's description of an invading human force.

With the War of Gog and Magog having begun shortly before the midpoint of the Tribulation, as revealed in the first four trumpets, it is likely the locusts of the fifth trumpet signify the continuation of this war involving Israel. Jesus warned, "when ye shall see Jerusalem compassed with armies, then know that the desolation thereof is nigh" (Luke 21:20). He goes on to say, "Then let them which are in Judaea flee to the mountains" (Luke 21:21). He also warns that Israel should flee to the mountains of Judea when the Antichrist declares himself God (Matt. 24:15–21), which takes place at precisely the midpoint of the Tribulation when Satan is cast to the earth and physically indwells the body of the Antichrist.

At the sounding of the sixth trumpet, the second "woe" judgment, the two hundred-million-man army from the East heads to Israel as part of the campaign of Armageddon. Just as a quarter of the earth's population will perish within the fourth seal judgment, an additional one-third of mankind will perish by fire, smoke, and brimstone within this sixth trumpet judgment (Rev. 9:13–19).

The holocaust of the fifth and sixth trumpets sets the stage for the seven bowls of wrath, which clearly describe the effects of radioactivity on man and his environment as a result of a nuclear exchange.

The seventh trumpet, and final "woe" judgment, is placed in time at the end of the seven-year Tribulation after the seven bowls of wrath. Regarding this seventh trumpet, Scripture says, "And the nations were angry, and thy wrath is come, and the time of the dead, that they should be judged, and that thou shouldest give reward unto thy servants the prophets, and to the saints, and them that fear thy name, small and great; and shouldest destroy them which destroy the earth" (Rev. 11:18).

With the sounding of the seventh trumpet, Jesus returns to earth to the battle of Armageddon to set up His millennial kingdom. But first, He must judge all who have survived the Tribulation, Jews and Gentiles alike. It is also at this time the Old Testament saints and all believers who died during the Tribulation face their day of judgment and reward. Therefore, the seventh trumpet depicts the Second Advent Resurrection and Judgment Program at the conclusion of the Tribulation.

Remember, by this point, it is only the believers from the Day of Pentecost to the Rapture, when Jesus removes the Church, who will have already faced judgment. There, believers will stand at the Judgment Seat of Christ to receive their rewards for faithful service while the Tribulation is taking place on earth. Scripture is clear: Every knee shall bow and every tongue confess that "Jesus Christ is Lord, to the glory of God the Father" (Phil. 2:10–11). So every person to ever live will stand before Him in judgment at one point or another. This resurrection and judgment program will be discussed at length as we progress chronologically through the Tribulation.

The Bowls of Wrath

The seven bowls of wrath are recorded in Revelation 16. By this point in the Tribulation, God has sent the 144,000 Jewish witnesses to evangelize to the world of the coming of Christ, His two special messengers preaching repentance specifically to Israel, and the three angels flying in midheaven, the first of whom preaches an eternal gospel "unto them that dwell on the earth, and to every nation, and kindred, and tongue, and people" (Rev. 14:6). The third angel even exhorts the inhabitants of the earth not to receive the Mark of the Beast or else they will seal their eternal destiny in the lake of fire (Rev. 14:9–11).

But Scripture warns, "Yea, they made their hearts as an adamant stone, lest they should hear the law, and the words which the LORD of hosts hath sent in his spirit by the former prophets: therefore came a great wrath from the LORD of hosts" (Zech. 7:12).

The bowls of wrath characterize the near destruction of mankind through the campaign of Armageddon. They depict the unrestrained fury of God upon a rebellious, sinful world at the end of the Great Tribulation. "Behold, the day of the LORD cometh, cruel both with wrath and fierce anger. . . . And I will punish the world for their evil, and the wicked for their iniquity. . . . I will make a man more precious than fine gold" (Isa. 13:9,11–12).

Again, as the seal judgments are an overview of the entire Tribulation, the bowls of wrath are incorporated within the sixth seal and also coincide with the fifth and sixth trumpets. In these bowls, we see the result of a nuclear holocaust which will involve all the nations of the world. Indeed, Scripture says, "I will gather all nations against Jerusalem to battle" (Zech. 14:2).

Now, let's quickly summarize the world's population at the time the bowls of wrath are poured out. At the Rapture, which commences the Tribulation, perhaps as many as a billion people will vanish worldwide. I hope that figure is far surpassed, but based on the apostasy of the Laodicean church age in which we live, we must be conservative here. Then at the War of Gog and Magog shortly before the midpoint of the Tribulation, as much as 1.5 billion people may perish, and then countless millions will die during the worldwide persecution of Christians and Jews at the hands of the Antichrist during the Great Tribulation.

So at the conclusion of the Great Tribulation, maybe two billion or so will remain, and we know from the sixth trumpet, which coincides with the bowls of wrath, that one-third of them will perish during the fiery holocaust of Armageddon (Rev. 9:15,18). Indeed, "except those days should be shortened, there should no flesh be saved" (Matt. 24:22). At this point, nearly all who remain will have accepted the Mark of the Beast, making them enemies of God, and He therefore "reserveth wrath for his enemies" (Nah. 1:2).

The first bowl of wrath produces "a noisome and grievous sore" on all who accept the Mark of the Beast (Rev. 16:2). Though redemption is now too late for them, one would think after all that has taken place up to this point in the Tribulation, they would fall on their faces and beg forgiveness of Almighty God. Instead, Scripture says, "they gnawed their tongues for pain, And blasphemed the God of heaven because of their pains and their sores, and repented not of their deeds" (Rev. 16:10–11).

The second bowl is poured out on the sea, again a likely reference to the Mediterranean Sea, turning it to blood and killing every living thing therein. Likewise, the third bowl turns the rivers and springs of waters to blood. The reference to "blood" is symbolic of the contamination of these waters as a result of radioactivity. When we look back at the trumpets, Scripture says, "there fell a great star from heaven, burning as it were a lamp, and it fell upon the third part of the rivers, and upon the fountains of waters; And the name of the star is called Wormwood: and the third part of the waters became wormwood; and many men died of the waters, because they were made bitter" (Rev. 8:10–11). Clearly, the "great star" depicts a nuclear missile, which indeed matches the description of a burning torch flying through the air. The name "Wormwood" is yet unclear and will only be revealed over time, but today, in the vast array of military arsenal, there are currently warheads known as "Silkworm" missiles. Therefore, the second and third bowls of wrath kill every living thing in the Mediterranean Sea and all who drink of the rivers and springs in that region (Rev. 16:6; cf. Rev. 17:6).

The fourth bowl causes the sun "to scorch men with fire" and "great heat." For those of us who live in the South, summers *do* feel like the fourth bowl of wrath, but even the hottest of our summers cannot compare to this extreme heat. The ozone layer, which surrounds the planet in the upper atmosphere, protects us from the harmful effects of the sun. If it were compressed and brought down to sea level, it would only be an eighth of an inch thick. When radioactivity is unleashed into the atmosphere, it will destroy this delicate, protective layer, causing the sun to scorch men "with great heat." Yet incredibly, they "blasphemed the name of God . . . and they repented not to give him glory" (Rev. 16:9).

The fifth bowl of wrath is poured out "upon the seat of the beast," and, it says, "his kingdom was full of darkness" (Rev. 16:10). Here we see a darkening over Israel from the nuclear fallout of Armageddon. We know this is Israel because "the seat of the beast" depicts the throne in the Third Temple, which is to be built in Jerusalem by the midpoint of the Tribulation. The Antichrist, also known as the beast, will defile the Temple by sitting on the throne and declaring himself God (2 Thess. 2:4).

The sixth bowl of wrath dries up the great Euphrates River, enabling the two hundred-million-man army from the East to successfully cross over (Rev. 16:12). This may be as a result of the intense, scorching heat of the fourth bowl of wrath, or it may be the result of man's intervention. Today, the Arab nation of Turkey controls the giant Ataturk Dam which regulates the flow of water into the Euphrates River. They may therefore assist the invading force from the East in their march through the desert and into the Holy Land.

Finally the seventh bowl of wrath depicts demons going "forth unto the kings of the earth and of the whole world, to gather them to the battle of that great day of God Almighty" (Rev. 16:14). These demons are instrumental in leading all the nations of the world to converge on Israel "into a place called in the Hebrew tongue Armageddon" (Rev. 16:16).

Chapter 7

The Seven-Year Tribulation
(Daniel's Seventieth Week)

THE TRIBULATION WILL BEGIN immediately following the Rapture. It is the final seven years of civilization as we know it. To better understand this, we must defer to the prophet Daniel, who recorded Israel's future through a period of seventy "weeks" of years (Dan. 9:24–27).

In 538 B.C., while in Babylonian captivity, Daniel read Jeremiah's prophecy of Israel's captivity in Babylon lasting for seventy years. He also discovered that afterward, the Jews would return to their homeland (Jer. 25:11; 29:10). Daniel realized sixty-seven of the seventy years had already passed, and he began a lengthy intercessory prayer for the restoration and deliverance of the Jews from their captivity.

While he was praying, the Lord sent the angel Gabriel to reveal to Daniel the future of the Jewish people. Gabriel announced, "Seventy weeks are determined upon thy people and upon thy holy city, to finish the transgression, and to make an end of sins, and to make reconciliation for iniquity, and to bring in everlasting righteousness, and to seal up the vision and prophecy, and to anoint the most Holy" (Dan. 9:24). In this passage, the Hebrew word for "weeks" is *shabua*, meaning "seven." Therefore, the total time of "seventy weeks" for Israel's future would be four hundred ninety years, or seventy times seven. Gabriel goes on to say the seventy weeks would be borne out in three segments of time, which would begin immediately upon the decree to restore and rebuild Jerusalem (Dan. 9:25–26).

The first time period given is seven weeks, or forty-nine years. In 445 B.C., nearly a hundred years after Gabriel revealed Israel's future events to Daniel, Artaxerxes Longimanus issued the decree to restore and rebuild Jerusalem (Neh. 2:4–8). This marked the point at which Israel's seventy weeks, or 490 years, would begin to count down.

The second time period given is sixty-two weeks, or four hundred thirty-four years. This period began at the conclusion of the first period and ended on Palm Sunday when the Lord Jesus rode into Jerusalem on a donkey. He was rejected by the Jews as their King and Messiah and crucified that following Friday. Even as Jesus approached Jerusalem, He knew He would be rejected. He prophesied of His rejection in a parable of the nobleman who was leaving to a distant country to receive his kingdom. The nobleman is symbolic of Jesus. "But his citizens hated him, and sent a message after him, saying, We will not have this man to reign over us" (Luke 19:14). The Jews were expecting their King to be a mighty conqueror, not a lowly carpenter. They failed to see the coming of the Messiah first, as sacrifice, then as conquering King.

So we have the first period of seven weeks and the second period of sixty-two weeks, bringing the total time of Israel's history to sixty-nine weeks, or four hundred eighty-three years. However, when the Lord Jesus was rejected by the Jews, Israel's prophetic time clock abruptly stopped, with seven years remaining to complete Gabriel's prophecy of four hundred ninety years. God then gave the Jews "the spirit of slumber, eyes that they should not see, and ears that they should not hear" (Rom. 11:8). The apostle Paul wrote, "blindness in part is happened to Israel, until the fulness of the Gentiles be come in" (Rom. 11:25). The Jews were the chosen of God to bring the message of salvation to the whole world, but when they rejected their Messiah, God directed His attention to the Gentiles to bring the message of salvation, and thus began the Church age. For nearly two thousand years, the Church has been the focus of God's redemptive activity. Just as Israel's prophetic time clock stopped at the birth of the Church, the removal of the Church at the Rapture will resume it. At that point, God will then redirect His focus to the Jews for the remaining seven years of Gabriel's prophecy, or Daniel's Seventieth Week.

Contrary to popular belief, the Tribulation is not a period of time set aside for God to vent His anger on mankind for His thousands of years of suppressed anger due to our sin and rebellion. Some parents might do so under the same circumstances, but our loving and patient Father is not like that. This will be the worst time in human history, but not because God is "getting even" with man.

While God will purge the earth of sin during the Tribulation and judge its political and religious systems, its primary purpose is to prepare the Jews for the Messiah who is coming to fulfill God's Word. Jesus will return to earth at the end of the Tribulation to establish His millennial reign in fulfillment of three covenants made by God for the nation of Israel. Though the earth and nearly all of its inhabitants will be destroyed, a remnant of *Jews and Gentiles* will enter the Millennium in their physical bodies as the recipients of God's unconditional promises made to Abraham and his seed thousands of years ago. Paul wrote, "There is neither Jew nor Greek, there is neither bond nor free, there is neither male nor female: for ye are all one in Christ Jesus. And if ye be Christ's, then are ye Abraham's seed, and heirs according to the promise" (Gal. 3:28–29). So Gentiles are also recipients of the covenants promised to Abraham, but events of the Tribulation will be centered around the Jews and the nation of Israel.

God made three unconditional covenants with Israel which have not yet been fulfilled. Their fulfillment is mandatory based on the character and integrity of God. God is incapable of untruths or broken promises, and when He makes a covenant, it will absolutely be fulfilled. "My covenant will I not break, nor alter the thing that is gone out of my lips" (Ps. 89:34). Thus, the preparatory seven-year Tribulation is primarily to usher in the millennial reign of Christ in fulfillment of God's covenants to His people.

The first of three yet-to-be-fulfilled covenants is found in the book of Genesis. There we find the Abrahamic covenant where God promised Abraham his descendants would occupy all the land of Canaan. God told him, "For all the land which thou seest, to thee will I give it, and to thy seed for ever" (Gen. 13:15). God also promised him the number of his descendants would be "as the stars of the heaven, and as the sand which is upon the sea shore" (Gen. 22:17). Additionally, God promised in Abraham's seed "shall all families of the earth be blessed," that his descendants will be "as the dust of the earth: so that if a man can number the dust of the earth, then shall [his] seed also be numbered" (Gen. 12:3; 13:16). This covenant will be fulfilled during Christ's millennial reign on earth.

The second yet-to-be-fulfilled promise of God is the Palestinic covenant, as recorded in the book of Deuteronomy. Through this covenant, God promised that Israel would fully repent, that all would be converted, and that the Lord would return and restore them to their land (Deut. 30:1–10). It also provides the basis upon which the land of Canaan will someday be occupied by Abraham's descendants.

Finally, the third yet-to-be-fulfilled promise of God is the Davidic covenant, as recorded in the books of Second Samuel, Jeremiah, and the Psalms. In the Davidic covenant, God promised David a son who would be a king: Solomon. But

God also promised in David's seed an eternal throne and an everlasting kingdom would be established, that of the Lord Jesus.

Though the horrors of the Tribulation focus on the nations of Israel, God assures them, "Like as I have brought all this great evil upon this people, so will I bring upon them all the good that I have promised them" (Jer. 32:42). Christ's millennial kingdom will fulfill all the covenants He has made with His people. The secondary purpose for the Tribulation is *then* to purge the earth of sin and rebellion.

The Tribulation must be seen in three sections: the first half, the midpoint, and the second half. Each half totals forty-two months, with each month lasting thirty days. Therefore, each half contains exactly twelve hundred sixty days, or three and one-half years, with the two halves totaling seven years. At the midpoint, a pivotal event takes place commencing the second half of the Tribulation, which is referred to as the Great Tribulation. It will be a perilous time, to which the prophet Jeremiah referred as like unto "the time of Jacob's trouble" (Jer. 30:7), indeed one in which Jesus warned "such as was not since the beginning of the world to this time, no, nor ever shall be" (Matt. 24:21).

The Oslo Peace Accord

On September 13, 1993, after two years of U.S.-brokered negotiations, the late Israeli prime minister Yitzhak Rabin, PLO leader Yasser Arafat, and U.S. president Bill Clinton shook hands in agreement over what were then acceptable peace terms between the history-long rivals. Among its declarations, the Oslo Peace Accord stipulated Israel would trade six major towns in the West Bank, including Jericho, to the Palestinians in exchange for peace.

Politicians applauded and people the world over celebrated, but many in Israel did not. They viewed the agreement as the Palestinians taking one step closer to making good on their threats to wipe them out. In fact, Yasser Arafat once said, "Peace for us means the destruction of Israel." So his signature across a document meant nothing to them. Clearly, the less land Israel has, the more vulnerable they are to attack.

This fact did not go unnoticed by one Jewish student named Yigal Amir. On November 4, 1995, ironically the night Yitzhak Rabin was attending a peace rally in Tel Aviv, the young student opened fire on the prime minister, killing him. Rabin had previously signed a peace accord with the late King Hussein of Jordan in October of 1994 and was in negotiations with Syrian president Hafez Assad over trading the Golan Heights for peace, the strategic mountainous territory located between northern Israel and Syria. Rabin's death halted the process, but not Syria's desire for the land. The *Jerusalem Post* in August of 1997 quoted Syrian chief of staff Hikhmat Shihabi as saying they would "take back the Golan Heights by force if it cannot do so peacefully." Without the Heights, Israel would be defenseless against an invading foe from the north. Notwithstanding, they will likely relinquish this territory since Scripture warns of an invading force from the north coming against the mountains of Israel (Ezek. 39:2).

The assassination of Yitzhak Rabin was critical to end-time events. Rabin mistakenly believed that by trading land for peace, Israel would somehow satisfy her Arab neighbors. But the Arabs are committed, even to the point of death, to the eradication of the Jews in the Middle East. In so doing, the Arabs are fulfilling an ordinance of the Muslim faith and thereby pleasing Allah, their god. In the prophetical scheme of things, Rabin had to die to prepare the way for Israel's next prime minister, Benjamin Netanyahu, a man faithfully devoted to seeing the Jews retain the territory promised them by God.

Because of violence and constant terrorist attacks, the peace process stalled for nineteen months, but realizing the urgency of the impending deadline, the Middle East leaders reconvened in October of 1998 at the Wye River Plantation in Maryland in an attempt to resume the peace process. After nine days of intense negotiations, an agreement was finally reached on October 23, 1998, in what is now referred to as the Wye Accord. The terms of this treaty revolve around implementation of the Oslo Accord.

Once again, the world applauded as efforts for peace in the Mideast seemed underway, but the accord has proven to be disastrous, with problem upon problem and little being done to resume the process at all. Netanyahu's agreement to cede an additional thirteen percent of the West Bank to the Palestinians came as a surprise to even his most staunch supporters. Living among 1.5 million Palestinians, the one hundred fifty thousand Israeli settlers in the West Bank felt their leader betrayed them, and they stood resistant to the accord, staging continual protests. As well, hardliners within the Israeli and Palestinian cabinets rejected the accord, prompting U.S. negotiators to feverishly work toward resolving the issues before the May 4, 1999, expiration of the Oslo Accord.

The European Union's absence in the Wye Accord peace talks hardly went unnoticed. In May of 1998, the EU hosted a peace summit in London for the Middle East leaders, acting as the Palestinian's representative, while the U.S. acted on behalf of Israel. In April of 1998, one month prior to the London summit, Yasser Arafat stated at a press conference, "Our position has always been that the European Union must have a vital, effective role in this peace process." Yet in the Wye River Plantation meeting held only five months later, the EU was nowhere to be found. The terms of the Wye Accord established a land-for-security deal in which Israel demanded a guarantee of security from Palestinians against terrorist attacks before they would relinquish territory in the West Bank. But so far, the agreement has proven to be something the Palestinians cannot enforce, and the situation continues to escalate.

Indeed, the EU will prove to have a vital role in the peace process, acting on behalf of the Palestinians to guarantee Israel's security. A man is about to emerge from within the EU who will have the perfect solution, giving the Arabs the land they want, yet promising Israel the peace she so desperately seeks. Richard Nixon once said, "The greatest honor history can bestow is that of a peacemaker." According to the Scriptures, a peacemaker is definitely on the horizon, but hardly one in whom honor can be bestowed.

The First Three and One-Half Years

Anyone who relies on outside security will be committing suicide.
—David Bar Illam, Senior Policy Advisor to Former Israeli Prime Minister Benjamin Netanyahu CNN World News, May 14, 1998

The Tribulation begins following the Rapture of the Church. Immediately, 144,000 Jews throughout the world will accept Christ and begin evangelizing, telling of His imminent return, and the need for repentance. The conversion of these Jews will likely stem from a supernatural event, much like the apostle Paul's conversion to Christianity while on the road to Damascus (Acts 9). As well, God's Two Witnesses will begin their ministry in Israel for exactly twelve hundred sixty days, or the entirety of the first half of the Tribulation. These two men will come in judgment, causing drought, famine, and plagues on the earth, yet unceasingly preaching repentance. They will be hated by the world because of the torment they inflict (Rev. 11). On the political scene, Israel will secure her long-awaited peace, while a false religious figure known as the False Prophet will surface to exalt the man who made it happen.

As well, an apostate religious system known as "the great harlot" will begin to emerge. This includes the professing church, those who claimed to be saved when they were not and, as such, were left behind at the Rapture. These are the ones of which Jesus spoke when He said, "Not every one that saith unto me, Lord, Lord, shall enter into the kingdom of heaven; but he that doeth the will of my Father which is in heaven. Many will say to me in that day, Lord, Lord, have we not prophesied in thy name? and in thy name have cast out devils? and in thy name done many wonderful works? And then will I profess unto them, I never knew you: depart from me, ye that work iniquity" (Matt. 7:21–23).

At the outset of the Tribulation, the crisis in the Middle East over the Oslo Peace Accord will immediately be resolved by a man emerging out of Europe, the Antichrist. Scripture says, "he shall confirm the covenant with many for one week" (Dan. 9:27). The word "confirm" means to "ratify," "strengthen," or "make firm," which necessarily denotes a covenant, or agreement, which has already been established. He will simply uphold the terms and conditions of a preceding treaty, those of the Oslo Peace Accord. The reference to "week" is to Daniel's Seventieth Week, the Tribulation.

As leader of a member nation in the European Union, the Antichrist will somehow convince Israel that their security can rest in this powerful bloc of nations to protect them. After all, the European Union currently includes fifteen member nations, totaling nearly half a billion people, and boasts of a combined gross domestic product of $6.5 trillion, making them the most powerful economic force in the world.

Presumably then, if the EU, as the Palestinians' representative, guarantees Israel's security, they will feel confident to let down their guard.

In fact, that is exactly what they will do. Israel will agree to the terms of the covenant confirmed by the Antichrist. His promise of guaranteed peace will lull them into a false sense of security, for they are seen living in a "land of unwalled villages," people "that are at rest, that dwell safely, all of them dwelling without walls, and having neither bars nor gates" (Ezek. 38:11).

Their peaceful occupation will be shortlived, however. Like *everything* out of Satan's mouth, the promise will be a lie, a false covenant. The prophet Isaiah wrote of this, stating, "We have made a covenant with death, and with hell are we at agreement" (Isa. 28:15). He goes on to say, "for we have made lies our refuge, and under falsehood have we hid ourselves." Jeremiah wrote of this same covenant, "They have healed also the hurt of the daughter of my people slightly, saying, Peace, peace; when there is no peace" (Jer. 6:14). The Antichrist, through the European Union, will guarantee Israel's security, enabling them to live in peace, but he will betray the Jews by breaking the treaty three and one-half years later (Dan. 9:27).

The Revived Roman Empire

Over twenty-five hundred years ago, Nebuchadnezzar, king of Babylon, had a troubling dream. When he awoke, he had forgotten what the dream was, yet he wanted an explanation. He summoned magicians, conjurers, sorcerers, and astrologers to, first, tell him the dream, and then interpret its meaning. Of course, no one was able. So he ordered all the wise men of Babylon killed, including the prophet Daniel, who was being held in captivity. When Daniel found out what was going on, he asked to interpret the dream for the king, and permission was granted. God then revealed the dream to Daniel in a vision (Dan. 2).

Nebuchadnezzar had seen into the future. He saw a great statue standing in front of him with a head of fine gold, its chest and arms of silver, its belly and thighs of bronze, its legs of iron, with the feet and toes partly of iron and clay. In the interpretation of the dream, the statue represented four kingdoms or empires which would rule successively over the entire earth.

The head of gold represented the mighty Babylonian Empire with Nebuchadnezzar as king. The chest and arms of silver represented the Medo-Persian Empire under Darius and Cyrus the Persian. The belly and thighs of bronze represented the Grecian Empire under Alexander the Great. And, lastly, the legs of iron, along with the feet and toes partly of iron and clay, represented the fourth world-ruling kingdom, the mighty Roman Empire (Dan. 2).

Later, the prophet Daniel saw a vision which paralleled Nebuchadnezzar's dream of four world-ruling empires. However, in Daniel's vision, the empires are characterized by four voracious beasts (Dan. 7). The first three beasts are described as a lion with eagle's wings, a bear with a paw raised and three ribs in its mouth, and a four-headed leopard with wings of a fowl on its back. Yet the fourth beast is described differently. It is depicted as exceedingly dreadful, extremely strong, terrifying, having large iron teeth and claws of bronze. The beast had ten horns with an additional "little horn" coming up from among them. The "little horn" is described as having "eyes like the eyes of man, and a mouth speaking great things" (Dan. 7:8).

Daniel sought the meaning of the vision. He was told, "These great beasts, which are four, are four kings, which shall arise out of the earth" (Dan. 7:17). But he was particularly disturbed by the fourth beast and wanted to know the exact meaning of it. He was told, "The fourth beast shall be the fourth kingdom upon earth, which shall be diverse from all kingdoms, and shall devour the whole earth, and shall tread it down, and break it in pieces. And the ten horns out of this kingdom are ten kings that shall arise: and another shall rise after them; and he shall be diverse from the first, and he shall subdue three kings" (Dan. 7:23–24).

As sure as it is written in God's Word, it will come to pass. As a matter of fact, the phrase "come (or came) to pass" is mentioned in the Scriptures more than six hundred times. From Daniel's vision onward, history records the four world-ruling kingdoms began with the Babylonian Empire, spanning from 605 B.C. to 539 B.C.; the Medo-Persian Empire, from 539 B.C. to 331 B.C.; the Grecian Empire, from 331 B.C. to 242 B.C.; and finally the Roman Empire, which initially conquered Sicily in 242 B.C., and subsequently the remainder of the Mediterranean world. The Roman Empire, however, was never conquered by an invading force. As the centuries passed, the power and glory of the fourth world-ruling empire simply diminished. Finally, in A.D. 476, Rome fell, only existing thereafter as a religious empire.

But Daniel recorded ten kings as part of the fourth and final world-ruling empire, as does the book of Revelation. "And the ten horns which thou sawest are ten kings, which have received no kingdom as yet; but receive power as kings one hour with the beast. These have one mind, and shall give their power and strength unto the beast" (Rev. 17:12–13). Ten kings have never ruled simultaneously within the ancient Roman Empire. It must therefore necessitate a *revived* formation, characterized by an alliance of ten nations.

Most students of prophecy agree that the powerful European Union represents the revived Roman Empire. Without question, it is *the* foremost economic bloc in the world. However, the EU currently has fifteen member nations with dozens slated to follow, leaving us to speculate on a reformation of the European Union. But Daniel wrote, *"out of this kingdom* are ten kings that shall arise" (Dan. 7:24, italics mine). In other words, out of the European Union as the revived Roman Empire, ten kings will arise.

So much focus has been on the European Union that few have noticed the ten-nation alliance of the Western European Union. In fact, the WEU is the *defense* arm of the European Union and the division through which guarantees of security can be made. The Maastricht Declarations established in December 1991, state: "The Western European Union will be developed as the defense component of the European Union and as the means to strengthen the European pillar of the Atlantic Alliance. To this end, it will formulate a common European defense policy and carry forward its concrete implementation through the further development of its own operational role."

So at the outset of the Tribulation, a man will arise out of the ten-nation Western European Union, the defense arm of the powerful EU. He will confirm the Oslo Peace Accord, giving the Palestinians the land they want, while guaranteeing Israel their security. As such, for nearly three and one-half years after the Tribulation begins, with the Arab/Israeli conflict seemingly resolved, the world will experience relative peace, yet at the same time suffer terribly through drought, famine, and plagues wrought by God's Two Witnesses, whose ministry of judgment lasts until the midpoint. All the while, the 144,000 Jewish evangelists will faithfully proclaim the name of Jesus, turning the hearts of countless millions to Christ. It is also within this time that a false religious figure will emerge, the False Prophet, who will perform many miraculous signs and point the way to the Antichrist as God. As well, the apostate church known as the "great harlot" will emerge.

The Third Jewish Temple

After the Rapture of the Church and by the midpoint of the Tribulation, the Third Jewish Temple will be built in Jerusalem (Dan. 9:25; Zech. 1:14–16; 2 Thess. 2:4; Rev. 11:1–2). No doubt the Antichrist's influence over the Palestinians will make this a possibility. According to Jewish law, the Temple must be built on the original site of Solomon's Temple. Known as the Temple Mount, this thirty-five–acre tract of land is undoubtedly the most volatile piece of property in the world. It currently houses two of Islam's holiest shrines, the Al Aqsa Mosque and the Dome of the Rock, yet the Third Jewish Temple is to be built there, causing a major problem between the two faiths.

In the late 1990s, the Temple Mount Faithful, a Jewish group dedicated to the construction of the Temple, actually attempted to begin construction by laying its four-ton cornerstone. This enraged the Palestinians and a riot ensued thereafter in which seventeen people were killed. Once again, in October of 1998, the Temple Mount Faithful set out to lay the cornerstone. This time the hopeful group was stopped by angry Palestinians without violence. Needless to say, the Antichrist must be instrumental in controlling the peace and allowing this event to take place.

The First Jewish Temple was built by King Solomon. It was known for its lavish beauty more than its great size. It was destroyed in 586 B.C. when the Babylonians under King Nebuchadnezzar burned Jerusalem. Later, under Zerubbabel, Jewish exiles of the Babylonian captivity returned to their homeland and built the Second Temple, completing its modest structure in 516 B.C.

Nearly five hundred years later, in 20 B.C., Herod the Great began a massive renovation of the Temple. A tireless builder, his decision to renovate was motivated only by the desire to bring prestige unto himself. However, he died before its completion, and in A.D. 64, under King Herod Agrippa II, the brilliant twenty-six–acre, white marble structure was fully completed, eighty-four years after construction initially began. Six years later, in A.D. 70, all but the western wall of the Temple was totally destroyed when the Roman general Titus conquered Jerusalem. We know it today as the Wailing Wall where Orthodox Jews gather to pray for the Temple's restoration.

In anticipation of the construction of the Temple, preparation for Temple worship has long been underway. For nearly twenty years, rabbis at the Temple Institute in Jerusalem have been preparing Jewish students from the priestly tribe of Levi in the knowledge and fulfillment of their duties once the Temple is completed. Over eighty objects and utensils, including musical instruments of the Bible, have currently been replicated for Temple service.

Of much significance to the rebuilding of the Temple and the resumption of Temple worship is the search for the perfect red heifer. In Numbers 19, an ordinance was established by God for the purification of sin before entry into the Temple. A perfect, unblemished red heifer is to be sacrificed and its ashes mixed with spring water to cleanse the high priest from sin.

In June of 1997, CNN reported the perfect red heifer had been born on a farm in northern Israel. Dubbed "Melody," the red heifer instigated a swarm of controversy between Jews and Arabs and ignited apocalyptic fervor the world over. Arabs feared the discovery would signal the construction of the Third Temple. But despite all the excitement, in January of 1998 it was determined that Melody had failed the test of perfection when her owner discovered white hairs in her tail, rendering her an unacceptable sacrifice.

Famed archaeologist Vendyl Jones believes the ashes of the red heifer lie in a cave north of Qumran, the cave in which the Dead Sea Scrolls were discovered in 1947. Qumran is also near a spring of fresh water known as Ain Feshkha. Jones has been digging for the ashes since 1977.

Along with the ashes of the perfect red heifer, there are two other essential components to the resumption of Temple worship: the oil and the incense (Exod. 30:22–38). The holy oil must be of precise ingredients as established by God. It was used to anoint the priests for service, as well as the Temple structure with its many utensils and furnishings. The incense must also be of precise ingredients as established by God.

Incredibly, in 1988, Vendyl Jones and his excavating team unearthed a container of oil which, upon further examination, matched the ingredients of the holy anointing oil needed for Temple worship. Later, in May of 1992, they discovered a trough containing a red substance which also matched the ingredients of the incense.

Though it would be a thrilling discovery to find the Ark of the Covenant, it is not required to resume Temple worship. It was certainly not present at the Second Temple, which the Jews built after returning from Babylonian captivity. In fact, the Ark has been missing for nearly three thousand years, and its location still remains a mystery. But recent word out of Israel is that Vendyl Jones may be close to discovering its whereabouts as well.

When the Jews recaptured Jerusalem in the Six-Day War of 1967, the event which marked the "budding of the fig tree," Jewish historian Israel Eldad made this incredible statement: "We are at the stage at which David was when he liberated Jerusalem. From that time until the construction of the Temple by Solomon, only one generation passed. So will it be with us."[1]

Clearly, the Third Jewish Temple will be built *by* the midpoint of the Tribulation, for there will be the cessation of Temple worship rituals at that time. "And he shall confirm the covenant with many for one week: and in the midst of the week he shall cause the sacrifice and the oblation to cease" (Dan. 9:27).

The War of Gog and Magog

Nearly twenty-six hundred years ago, the prophet Ezekiel warned of a mighty military force that would someday invade Israel (see Ezek. 38–39). This invasion is referred to as the War of Gog and Magog, and it begins shortly before the midpoint of the Tribulation. It is the first in a series of battles that will extend over the entire second half of the Tribulation. In the book of Revelation, the battle of Armageddon is referred to as "the battle of that great day of God Almighty" (Rev. 16:14). The Greek word used for "battle" in this passage is *polemos*, meaning "war" or "campaign," while *mache* signifies "a battle," and in certain cases single combat. The War of Gog and Magog begins the campaign of warfare, culminating with the battle of Armageddon at the end of the Tribulation.[2]

During the War of Gog and Magog, three movements into Palestine will occur. Scripture warns, "And at the time of the end shall the king of the south push at him: and the king of the north shall come against him" (Dan. 11:40). Shortly before the midpoint of the Tribulation, an invading force will enter Israel from the south. Because the Antichrist, through a federation of ten nations, has promised to protect Israel, he and his forces will then move into Palestine. While this is taking place, an alliance of nations will then invade Israel from the north. Remember, this campaign will begin shortly before the midpoint of the Tribulation. By this point, the Antichrist has not yet ascended to world ruler. He is still the leader of a single European nation.

The King of the South. Throughout Scripture, Egypt is commonly referred to as the land of the South. Egypt will likely make the first move in the war, sending its forces into Israel to attack Jerusalem.

The Antichrist and His Army. Because the Antichrist has promised to protect Israel through his ten-nation federation, when the Egyptian forces invade Israel, he will come to her defense and move his army into Palestine.

Incredibly, in October of 1998, British prime minister Tony Blair announced plans for developing a European Union army within NATO, one in which joint military operations would be permitted between member nations of the EU and facilitated through the Western European Union, the defense arm of the EU as established under the terms of the Maastricht Treaty. Blair cited a need for the EU to have its own military "identity," allowing them to stage and oversee peacekeeping missions in Europe without having to consult other members of NATO. The United States has given its approval to the plan.

The King of the North. At about the same time, an assembly of nations will invade Israel from the north. Because this massive force enters Israel from the north, the entire alliance is referred to as the Northern Confederacy or the Northern Alliance. Scripture warns, "And thou shalt come from thy place out of the north parts, thou, and many people with thee . . . a great company, and a mighty army: And thou shalt come up against my people of Israel, as a cloud to cover the land" (Ezek. 38:15–16). The leader of the Northern Confederacy is referred to as Gog, the King of the North. He is not the Antichrist. They are two different individuals.

Gog is the chief prince of Rosh, Meshech, and Tubal from the land of Magog (Ezek. 38:2–3). Magog was the name of the second son of Japheth, who was the oldest son of Noah. Magog's descendants, the Scythians, inhabited the land north of the Black and Caspian seas, now modern-day Russia. Meshech and Tubal were also names of Japheth's sons.

Meshech speaks of Moscow, the capital of Russia, and Tubal of Tobolsk, the earliest province of Asiatic Russia to be colonized, while Rosh is believed to be another name for Russia.[3] When Gog invades Israel, he will bring all but a sixth of Russia with him in the invasion (Ezek. 39:2). Therefore, Russia will be the predominant force in the Northern Confederacy. At this very moment, events in Russia warn of the likely imminent return to militant communism.

A number of Arab and African nations will join Russia in this invasion into Palestine. The first alliance with Gog will be Persia (Ezek. 38:5), which is modern-day Iran. The second alliance will be Ethiopia (Ezek. 38:5). While the reference is apparent to the East African nation, there are eleven references in Scripture to Ethiopia as the land of Cush, which denotes at least a portion of Arabia. The third alliance with Gog will be Put (Ezek. 38:5). Its geographical location is widely accepted as the modern African nation of Libya. The fourth allied nation will be Gomer (Ezek. 38:6). Gomer was the name of another of Japheth's sons whose descendants were the Cimmerians occupying central Turkey during the Assyrian Empire. The reference to Gomer therefore likely depicts the nation of Turkey. The fifth Russian alliance will be Beth-togarmah (Ezek. 38:6). Togarmah was Japheth's grandson, the third son of Gomer. These descendants settled in the territory generally accepted as Armenia and may include certain Asiatic countries as well.[4] Finally, "many people" (Ezek. 38:6,15) will also align with this northern bloc of nations, but who they are remains to be seen.

For nearly three and one-half years into the Tribulation, the Jews will live securely in their own land by virtue of the Antichrist's guarantee of security. As leader of the ten-nation European alliance, the Antichrist will confirm a covenant with Israel, promising to protect the Jews from hostile Arab nations through the use of his own security forces. As such, Israel will be lulled into a false sense of security, not standing ready in her own defense. They are seen "at rest, that dwell safely, . . . without walls, and having neither bars nor gates" (Ezek. 38:11). Gog will consider them easy prey, and he and his alliance will therefore invade Israel from the north "to carry away silver and gold, to take away cattle and goods, to take a great spoil" (Ezek. 38:13).

The Outcome of the War. When the Egyptian forces enter Israel, the Antichrist and his army will move into Palestine to defend Israel. They will move downward into Egypt and collide with the advancing Egyptian army. At that point, Scripture says, "he shall have power over the treasures of gold and of silver, and over all the precious things of Egypt" (Dan. 11:43). The Antichrist and his forces will be victorious in the confrontation. "But tidings out of the east and out of the north shall trouble him: therefore he shall go forth with great fury to destroy, and utterly to make away many. And he shall plant the tabernacles of his palace between the seas in the glorious holy mountain" (Dan. 11:44–45). While they are subduing the Egyptian army, the Russian alliance will invade Israel from the north. The Antichrist and his forces will then make their headquarters in Jerusalem and prepare to go against the Northern Confederacy, but this time the Lord God will intervene on Israel's behalf.

Gog and his mighty military force will not prevail against Israel. Scripture says,

> And it shall come to pass at the same time when Gog shall come against the land of Israel, saith the Lord GOD, that my fury shall come up in my face. For in my jealousy and in the fire of my wrath have I spoken, Surely in that day there shall be a great shaking in the land of Israel; So that the fishes of the sea, and the fowls of the heaven, and the beasts of the field, and all creeping things that creep upon the

earth, and all the men that are upon the face of the earth, shall shake at my presence, and the mountains shall be thrown down, and the steep places shall fall, and every wall shall fall to the ground. And I will call for a sword against him throughout all my mountains, saith the Lord GOD: every man's sword shall be against his brother. And I will plead against him with pestilence and with blood; and I will rain upon him, and upon his bands, and upon the many people that are with him, and overflowing rain, and great hailstones, fire, and brimstone.

—Ezekiel 38:18–22

When Gog and his alliance invade Israel, Almighty God will fight against them using the forces of nature, combined with man-made weapons of destruction. In a parallel passage, Scripture says, "And the LORD shall cause his glorious voice to be heard, and shall shew the lighting down of his arm, with the indignation of his anger, and with the flame of a devouring fire, with scattering, and tempest, and hailstones . . . and in battles of shaking will he fight with it" (Isa. 30:30,32).

In another passage, Scripture says, "I will even rend it with a stormy wind in my fury; and there shall be an overflowing shower in mine anger, and great hailstones in my fury to consume it" (Ezek. 13:13). Again, "Upon the wicked he shall rain snares, fire and brimstone, and an horrible tempest: this shall be the portion of their cup" (Ps. 11:6).

That the invading force will perish by the sword is a clear indication of conventional warfare. Pestilence probably indicates biological warfare. Fire, brimstone, and burning wind are all components of nuclear activity. In fact, brimstone is actually sulphur and a component of chemical weapons. The torrential rains and hailstones will likely stem from a disruption of the atmosphere related to the intrusion of nuclear activity. During a nuclear explosion, the force of the blast compresses the atmosphere, pushing it into the upper layers of the stratosphere where the humid air is frozen and falls back to the earth in the form of giant hailstones.

Gog and his Northern Confederacy will be killed on the Golan Heights, the northern mountains of Israel. "Thou shalt fall upon the mountains of Israel, thou, and all thy bands, and the people that is with thee: I will give thee unto the ravenous birds of every sort, and to the beasts of the field to be devoured" (Ezek. 39:4). They "shall eat fat till [they] be full" (Ezek. 39:17–20). As many as 1.5 billion people may die in the conflict. It will take all of Israel seven months to bury the dead and seven years to dispose of the debris. They will be buried in what will be called the Valley of Hamongog, which means "the multitude of Gog" (Ezek. 39:9–12).

God will intervene on Israel's behalf to bring glory unto Himself. Scripture says, "And I will set my glory among the heathen, and all the heathen shall see my judgment that I have executed, and my hand that I have laid upon them. So the house of Israel shall know that I am the LORD their God from that day and forward" (Ezek. 39:21–22). Yet despite the defeat laden with miracles, the nations of the world will give the glory to the Antichrist. Gog's defeat will be attributed to the Antichrist's army moving against him, combined with the forces of nature.

This war will undoubtedly create world chaos and promote more of the New World Order propaganda, underscoring the need for a one-world government. Since the Antichrist upheld his promise to defend Israel in the name of peace, he will be perceived as a man of integrity and trustworthiness. From within his ten-nation federation, he will rapidly ascend in worldwide power. Regarding these ten nations, Scripture says, "These have one mind, and shall give their power and strength unto the beast" (Rev. 17:13).

Former Secretary General of NATO, Paul Henri Spaak, once said, "We do not want another committee; we have too many already. What we want is a man of sufficient stature to hold the allegiance of the people and to lift us out of the economic morass into which we are sinking. Send us such a man and be he god or devil, we will receive him."[5]

After all the conflict has ended, the Antichrist and his troops will continue to stay in Jerusalem, supposedly for her protection. By the midpoint of the Tribulation, he will be elevated to world ruler. Scripture says, "and all the world wondered after the beast . . . and they worshipped the beast, saying, Who is like unto the beast? who is able to make war with him?" (Rev. 13:3–4). He will remain in power as *world* ruler for the remainder of the Tribulation. "And power was given unto him to continue forty and two months . . . and power was given him over all kindreds, and tongues, and nations" (Rev. 13:5,7).

The Great Harlot Is Destroyed

For the first half of the Tribulation, this apostate religious system will permeate and influence the world (Rev. 17:2). It is described as "Babylon the great, the mother of harlots and abominations of the earth" (Rev. 17:5) because it characterizes the false religions which prevailed during the Babylonian era. This harlot religious system will threaten the agenda of the False Prophet, who has been pointing the way to the Antichrist as God. The ten nations and the beast will "hate the whore" and destroy her (Rev. 17:16) in order for the Antichrist to be the sole object of worship during the latter half of the Tribulation.

The Midpoint

Watch ye therefore, and pray always, that ye may be accounted worthy to escape all these things that shall come to pass, and to stand before the Son of man.

—Luke 21:36

Everything takes a drastic turn at this pivotal point in the Tribulation. A number of critical events will occur at this time. Initially, a seal will be supernaturally placed on the foreheads of the 144,000 Jewish evangelists to protect them from the horrors of the second half of the Tribulation (Rev. 7:1–8). As well, the three angels flying in midheaven will begin proclaiming their successive messages to the entire world (Rev. 14:6–11).

The Abomination of Desolation

Up to this point in the Tribulation, Satan has controlled the movements of the Antichrist and False Prophet. However, at precisely the midpoint, he will physically indwell the body of the Antichrist. Scripture warns, "Woe to the inhabiters of the earth and of the sea! for the devil is come down unto you, having great wrath, because he knoweth that he hath but a short time" (Rev. 12:12). As a result, the last half of the Tribulation "shall be a time of trouble, such as never was since there was a nation even to that same time" (Dan. 12:1). Only three and one-half years will remain until Jesus comes back to the earth.

Satan has always wanted to be God, but the most he will ever be is a pathetic fallen angel. In his five "I wills", he vowed to "ascend above the heights of the clouds; [he] will be like the most High" (Isa. 14:13–14), but as Beelzebub, he has ascended only as high as his name, which means "lord of the flies" (2 Kings 1:2). And the only throne he will ever temporarily sit on will be the throne in the Third Jewish Temple, which is why the Antichrist will be instrumental in seeing it constructed during the first three and one-half years of the Tribulation.

With his headquarters conveniently nestled in Jerusalem and his political position elevated to world ruler, when Satan indwells the Antichrist, he will lead him to betray Israel by breaking the peace treaty ratified with her three and one-half years earlier. Scripture says, "We looked for peace, but no good came; and for a time of health, and behold trouble! The snorting of his horses was heard from Dan: the whole land trembled at the sound of the neighing of his strong ones; for they are come, and have devoured the land, and all that is in it; the city, and those that dwell therein. For, behold, I will send serpents, cockatrices, among you, which will not be charmed, and they shall bite you, saith the LORD" (Jer. 8:15–17).

The Antichrist will put an abrupt end to sacrifices and grain offerings. He will then enter the Third Jewish Temple, seat himself on the throne, declare himself God, and demand the world worship him (Dan. 9:27; 2 Thess. 2:4). Of this act, the Abomination of Desolation, Jesus clearly warned. He said, "When ye therefore shall see the abomination of desolation, spoken of by Daniel the prophet, stand in the holy place . . . For then shall be great tribulation, such as was not since the beginning of the world to this time, no, nor ever shall be" (Matt. 24:15,21).

As history is destined to repeat itself, a similar event has previously occurred in Israel's history. According to the apocryphal books of 1 and 2 Maccabees, Antiochus Epiphanes, ruler of Syria from 175 to 164 B.C., once defiled the Jewish Temple. He hated the Jews and wanted to obliterate them from the face of the earth. In 168 B.C., he invaded Israel and entered the Temple in Jerusalem. He then put a stop to the sacrificial system of worship and desecrated the Temple by placing a pig on the altar and erecting a statue of a Greek pagan god in the Holy Place. According to Jewish law, a pig is an unclean animal for sacrifice, and by offering it on the altar, it rendered the Temple abominable. Thereupon ensued the Maccabean Revolt, led by Judas Maccabees, in which thousands of Jewish men, women, and children were killed.

Likewise, Satan hates God and the Jews and all who believe in Him. He hates the Jews because through them came the Savior, the Prophets, the Scripture, the Gospel, and the Church. After he indwells the Antichrist and seats himself on the throne of God, defiling the Temple like a big pig on the altar, he will begin his worldwide persecution of the Jews and all who have accepted Christ from the beginning of the Tribulation. "And when the dragon [Satan] saw that he was cast unto the earth, he persecuted the woman [Israel] which brought forth the man child. . . . And the dragon was wroth with the woman, and went to make war with the remnant of her seed, which keep the commandments of God, and have the testimony of Jesus Christ" (Rev. 12:13,17).

The Two Witnesses of God Killed
The first two people killed in the persecution will be the Two Witnesses of God. The Psalmist wrote, "in thy book all my members were written" (Ps. 139:16). Before we are even born, the number of our days are decreed, and when they are complete, God permits our deaths. Likewise, twelve hundred sixty days are allotted for the ministry of the Two Witnesses. "And when they shall have finished their testimony" the Antichrist himself will kill them (Rev. 11:7). He will not even afford them the dignity of a burial, but will instead order their bodies to be left in the streets of Jerusalem for all the world to see. No doubt this will be viewed on television sets around the world via satellite. Because of the droughts and plagues they inflict on the earth, people will celebrate their deaths and send each other gifts. This merriment is often called the devil's Christmas. But after three and one-half days, God will breathe life back into the Two Witnesses, and they will stand

to their feet. Can you imagine the looks on people's faces when they see these men come to life? Scripture says, "great fear fell upon them which saw them." God will then say, "Come up hither," and they will ascend into a cloud before the eyes of the whole world. At that point, an earthquake will take place in Jerusalem, where a tenth of the city will fall and seven thousand people will die, and "the remnant were affrighted, and gave glory to the God of heaven" (see Rev. 11:3–13).

The Mark of the Beast

Once the false religious figure known as the False Prophet emerges in the first half of the Tribulation, he will tirelessly point the way to the Antichrist as God. "He . . . causeth the earth and them which dwell therein to worship the first beast. . . . And he doeth great wonders, . . . And deceiveth them that dwell on the earth by the means of those miracles which he had power to do in the sight of the beast" (Rev. 13:12–14). Along with the False Prophet, the Antichrist will also perform miraculous signs. His deception "is after the working of Satan with all power and signs and lying wonders" (2 Thess. 2:9). When he seats himself on the throne in the Temple and declares himself God, the world will initially believe him.

The False Prophet will then tell those who dwell on the earth to make an image to the beast, and he will cause the image to speak and to kill all who do not worship the beast's image (Rev. 13:14–15). At the same time, he will administer a system whereby the "small and great, rich and poor, free and bond, [are] to receive a mark in their right hand, or in their foreheads" (Rev. 13:16). This is referred to as the Mark of the Beast. The mark may either be the Antichrist's name or the number of his name, which totals 6-6-6. Without it, no one can buy or sell or engage in any commerce whatsoever (Rev. 13:17–18).

While the Mark of the Beast is being administered throughout the world, the third angel flying in midheaven sternly warns against receiving the mark. He cries out, saying, "If any man worship the beast and his image, and receive his mark in his forehead, or in his hand, The same shall drink of the wine of the wrath of God, which is poured out without mixture into the cup of his indignation; and he shall be tormented with fire and brimstone in the presence of the holy angels, and in the presence of the Lamb: And the smoke of their torment ascendeth up for ever and ever: and they have no rest day nor night, who worship the beast and his image, and whosoever receiveth the mark of his name" (Rev. 14:9–11).

The mark must be received willingly; it will not be forced on anyone. But those who refuse to accept the mark will be beheaded. In the ancient Roman Empire, Christians were required to acknowledge "Caesar is Lord." The Caesars claimed to be gods. Those who refused, acknowledging "Jesus is Lord," did so at the cost of their lives. Not surprisingly, the same thing will occur under the Antichrist who emerges from a revised Roman Empire. John the apostle wrote, "I saw the souls of them that were beheaded for the witness of Jesus, and for the word of God, and which had not worshipped the beast, neither his image, neither had received his mark upon their foreheads, or in their hands" (Rev. 20:4).

Never in the history of mankind has a system of this nature been possible until now. With the use of computers and advanced scanning technology, the implementation of a barcoded mark or biochip placed under the skin is right around the corner. The biochips contain limitless information, such as your name, date of birth, Social Security number, all the pertinent information necessary to identify an individual or transact business. It is already suggested as a method for tracking children who are lost or abducted, and governments are even considering the use of such technology on parolees.

Animal clinics currently offer microchips as a means of easily locating a lost or stolen pet. The microchips are less than an inch long and contain all the pet's medical information, as well as the name and address of its owner. Regarding this technology, Tim Willard, executive officer of the World Future Society, recently made this prophetic statement: "The technology behind such a microchip is fairly uncomplicated, and with a little refinement, it could be used in a variety of human applications. Conceivably, a number could be assigned at birth and go with a person throughout life. At the checkout stand at the supermarket, you could simply pass your hand over a scanner and your bank account would automatically be debited."[6]

Biochips implanted in humans are currently in development and will be available soon. A shocking article in the May 7, 1996, edition of the *Chicago Tribune* confirmed, "A tiny chip implanted inside the human body to send and receive radio messages . . . is likely to be marketed as a consumer item early in the next century. Several technologies already available or under development will enable electronics firms to make implantable ID locators, say futurists, and our yearning for convenience and security makes them almost irresistible to marketers."[7]

While biochips are not used commercially yet, we are currently utilizing smart cards. A smart card is like a credit card, except it has a chip on the inside of it. Across America, Europe, and Japan, it is estimated there may be three to four billion in use today. Their current application is in pay phones, wireless phones, Internet access, banking, health care, and pay TV. Their benefits to include the ability to efficiently manage personal finance, reduce fraud, and eliminate the need to complete time-consuming forms. Just one card can access multiple services, networks, and the Internet.

Clearly, the administration of a worldwide monetary system has never been possible until today, and the Antichrist will avail himself of this technology. Over twenty years ago, Democratic senator Frank Church, chairman of a committee investigating activities of U.S. intelligence, stated, "The government has the technological capacity to impose 'total tyranny.' If ever a dictator came to power, there would be no place to hide."[8]

The Second Three and One-Half Years

And except those days should be shortened, there should no flesh be saved . . .

—Matthew 24:22

The prophet Jeremiah referred to this time as the "time of Jacob's trouble" (Jer. 30:7). "Jacob" refers to Israel. During this three and one-half–year period, two-thirds of the Jews in Israel will perish as a result of war and the Antichrist's persecution, but God has promised to bring a third of them through the fire (Zech. 13:8–9). Gentiles will also perish in the Antichrist's persecution. "A great multitude, which no man could number, of all nations, and kindreds, and people, and tongues . . . are they which came out of great tribulation" (Rev. 7:9,14).

All who die as a result of their faith in Christ during this time will sit on thrones and reign with Him for a thousand years in His millennial kingdom. John the apostle wrote, "I saw the souls of them that were beheaded for the witness of Jesus, and for the word of God, and which had not worshipped the beast, neither his image, neither had received his mark upon their foreheads, or in their hands; and they lived and reigned with Christ a thousand years. . . . They shall be priests of God and of Christ, and shall reign with him a thousand years" (Rev. 20:4,6).

The Kings of the East

"And the sixth angel poured out his vial upon the great river Euphrates; and the water thereof was dried up, that the way of the kings of the east might be prepared" (Rev. 16:12). A two hundred-million-man army from the East will cross the Euphrates River on their way into Palestine (Rev. 9:16). The river may be dried up supernaturally or as a result of man's intervention. As stated, the Turkish government controls the Ataturk Dam, which regulates the flow of water into the Euphrates River. As Turkey is predominantly an Arab nation, they may assist the invading army in their movement into Israel. While Red China currently boasts of a two hundred-million-man army, the reference is to "kings," plural. Therefore, a number of Asian nations will unite to challenge the worldwide authority of the Antichrist.

The Battle of Armageddon

As previously stated, in the passage referring to the battle of Armageddon (Rev. 16:14), the Greek word used for "battle" is *polemos*, meaning war or **campaign,** while *mache* only signifies a battle, and in certain cases single combat. Once the War of Gog and Magog begins, the campaign will extend over the second half of the Tribulation and culminate in the battle of Armageddon.

During this second half, the nations of the world will finally wake up and realize the man they elected to rule the world is, in fact, evil incarnate, and will begin to move against his headquarters in Jerusalem in an attempt to oust him from authority.

Shortly after the midpoint, the Asian alliance will begin their movement into Palestine. Then all the nations of the world will begin to gather in the Valley of Megiddo. "The kings of the earth and of the whole world . . . gather . . . to the battle of that great day of God Almighty . . . into a place called in the Hebrew tongue Armageddon" (Rev. 16:14,16). Though all the nations gather at Megiddo, the campaign of Armageddon covers the entire land of Palestine, from the plains of Esdraelon on the north (Rev. 16:16; Judg. 4,5,7; 1 Sam. 31:8; 2 Kings 9:27; 23:29–30), down through Jerusalem (Zech. 12:2–11; 14:2), extending out to the valley of Jehoshaphat on the east (Joel 3:2,13; Ezek. 39:11), and to Edom on the south (Isa. 34,63).

The prophet Joel describes this convergence of armies into Israel. He wrote, "as the morning spread upon the mountains: a great people and a strong; there hath not been ever the like, neither shall be any more after it, even to the years of many generations" (Joel 2:2). The prophet Ezekiel likens the number of troops to "a cloud to cover the land" (Ezek. 38:9,16). In fact, blood will reach to the horses' bridles for a distance of two hundred miles (Rev. 14:20), which covers most of the land of Israel from north to south.

There is little question that nuclear weapons will be used at Armageddon. A nuclear fallout will darken the skies, just as the Scriptures repeatedly warn will occur. "A day of darkness and of gloominess, a day of clouds and of thick darkness" (Joel 2:2). "Immediately after the tribulation of those days shall the sun be darkened, and the moon shall not give her light, and the stars shall fall from heaven, and the powers of the heavens shall be shaken" (Matt. 24:29). "That day is a day of wrath, a day of trouble and distress, a day of wasteness and desolation, a day of darkness and gloominess, a day of clouds and thick darkness" (Zeph. 1:15). "And it shall come to pass in that day, that the light shall not be clear, nor dark" (Zech. 14:6).

Chemical and biological weapons of mass destruction will also be used at Armageddon. Scripture indicates "a noisome and grievous sore" will develop on men's skin (Rev. 16:2). Anthrax causes boils and is a component of biological weapons. Nuclear warheads release radioactivity, and they will certainly cause malignant sores. Scripture gives this chilling account as well: "And this shall be the plague wherewith the LORD will smite all the people that have fought against Jerusalem; Their flesh shall consume away while they stand upon their feet, and their eyes shall consume away in their holes, and their tongue shall consume away in their mouth" (Zech. 14:12).

The prophet Isaiah wrote,

> Howl ye; for the day of the LORD is at hand; it shall come as a destruction from the Almighty. Therefore shall all hands be faint, and every man's heart shall melt: And they shall be afraid: pangs and sorrows shall take hold of them; they shall be in pain as a woman that travaileth: they shall be amazed one at another; their faces shall be as flames. Behold, the day of the LORD cometh, cruel both with wrath and fierce anger, to lay the land desolate: and he shall destroy the sinners thereof out of it. For the stars of heaven and the constellations thereof shall not give their light: the sun shall be darkened in his going forth, and the moon shall not cause her light to shine. And I will punish the world for their evil, and the wicked for their iniquity; and I will cause the arrogancy of the proud to cease, and will lay low the haughtiness of the terrible. I will make a man more precious than fine gold; even a man than the golden wedge of Ophir.
>
> —Isaiah 13:6–12

Finally, John the apostle described Armageddon as

> thunders, and lightnings; and there was a great earthquake, such as was not since men were upon the earth, so mighty an earthquake, and so great. And the great city [Jerusalem]

was divided into three parts, and the cities of the nations
fell: . . . And every island fled away, and the mountains
were not found. And there fell upon men a great hail out of
heaven, every stone about the weight of a talent: and men
blasphemed God because of the plague of the hail; for the
plague thereof was exceeding great.

—Revelation 16:18–21

A third of mankind will perish by fire, smoke, and brimstone
in this war of the great day of God, the Almighty (Rev. 9:15,18).
Though it is the final battle of the seven-year Tribulation, it is
not the final conflict of mankind, however. That will occur
when Satan is loosed at the conclusion of Christ's millennial
reign.

The Second Advent of Jesus Christ

"For I will gather all nations against Jerusalem to battle. . . .
In that day shall the LORD defend the inhabitants of Jerusalem. . . . Then shall the LORD go forth, and fight against those
nations, as when he fought in the day of battle" (Zech. 14:2;
12:8; 14:3).

Just as Israel is about to be annihilated, the resplendent
Lord Jesus will be seen "coming in the clouds of heaven with
power and great glory" (Matt. 24:30). He and the Church
will come together riding on white horses (Rev. 19:11,14).
He will also bring His holy angels with Him (Matt. 25:31;
2 Thess. 1:7–8). Israel will look up and see Jesus "whom they
have pierced, and they shall mourn for him, as one mour-
neth for his only son, and shall be in bitterness for him, as
one that is in bitterness for his firstborn" (Zech. 12:10). Imagine their shock, amazement, and heartbreak when Israel re-
alizes for the first time that they crucified their own Savior.

When the Lord returns, "his feet shall stand in that day
upon the mount of Olives, which is before Jerusalem on the

east, and the mount of Olives shall cleave in the midst thereof toward the east and toward the west, and there shall be a
very great valley; and half of the mountain shall remove toward the north, and half of it toward the south" (Zech. 14:4).
This relates to the great earthquake at Armageddon where
"the great city [Jerusalem] was divided into three parts" (Rev.
16:19). The glorious Lord Jesus is described as having eyes
as a flame of fire, wearing many crowns, and a name is written on Him which no one knows but Himself (Rev. 19:12),
and written across the thigh of His robe will be the words
"KING OF KINGS, AND LORD OF LORDS" (Rev. 19:16).

Incredibly, when the Lord appears, the Antichrist and all
the armies of the nations gathered in Israel will turn to fight
against Jesus and the saints and angels. "And I saw the beast,
and the kings of the earth, and their armies, gathered together to make war against him . . . and against his army" (Rev.
19:19).

It goes without saying our magnificent Lord and Savior
"shall overcome them: for he is Lord of lords, and King of
kings" (Rev. 17:14). The Antichrist and False Prophet will be
seized and thrown alive into the eternal lake of fire. "And the
beast was taken, and with him the false prophet. . . . These
both were cast alive into a lake of fire burning with brimstone. And the remnant were slain with the sword of him that
sat upon the horse" (Rev. 19:20–21). By the word of His mouth
He creates, and by the word of His mouth He destroys.

And as for Satan, he gets to twiddle his thumbs in the
abyss for a thousand years. "And I saw an angel come down
from heaven, having the key of the bottomless pit and a great
chain in his hand. And he laid hold on the dragon, that old
serpent, which is the Devil, and Satan, and bound him a thousand years, And cast him into the bottomless pit, and shut
him up, and set a seal upon him, that he should deceive the
nations no more, till the thousand years should be fulfilled"

(Rev. 20:1–3). As ruler of the demonic world, when Satan is bound, the demons will be subdued as well.

Satan will be taunted while he sits in the abyss. "Hell from beneath is moved for thee to meet thee at thy coming: it stirreth up the dead for thee, even all the chief ones of the earth; it hath raised up from their thrones all the kings of the nations. All they shall speak and say unto thee, Art thou also become weak as we? art thou become like unto us? Thy pomp is brought down to the grave, and the noise of thy viols: the worm is spread under thee, and the worms cover thee" (Isa. 14:9–11).

> *And the God of peace shall bruise Satan under your feet shortly . . .*
>
> **—Romans 16:20**

The Second Advent Resurrection and Judgment Program

As previously stated, the Tribulation is divided into two halves, each lasting exactly twelve hundred sixty days. But Daniel wrote that from when the Abomination of Desolation is set up, which is at the midpoint, there will be twelve hundred ninety days, and then he adds, "Blessed is he that waiteth, and cometh to the thousand three hundred and five and thirty days" (Dan. 12:11–12). The additional time amounts to seventy-five days, and it is placed after the battle of Armageddon but before the Millennium begins. Jesus said, "Behold, I come quickly; and my reward is with me, to give every man according as his work shall be" (Rev. 22:12). It is during this seventy-five–day period after the Second Advent that the resurrection and judgment program will take place.

It is hard to imagine how anyone will survive the Tribulation, but there will be a scant few from among Israel and the nations who will enter the Millennium in their physical state to receive the promises of God and to repopulate the earth.

But before Christ's righteous millennial reign can begin, it must be determined whether these people are saved because *no unsaved person* will enter the Millennium. Scripture is clear: "Verily, verily, I say unto thee, Except a man be born again, he cannot see the kingdom of God" (John 3:3). And again, "Except ye be converted . . . ye shall not enter into the kingdom of heaven" (Matt. 18:3). So at the end of the Tribulation, there will be the Judgment of Israel and the Judgment of Gentile Nations to determine salvation of those who survived. But first, there will be the resurrection of all the righteous from the beginning of Creation.

The Resurrection Program. The physical body of every person who has ever lived and died will someday be resurrected and reunited with their spirit. Some will come out of the grave to the resurrection of life, while others will come out of the grave to the resurrection of damnation. Once we reach the age of accountability, an age which only God knows, we are responsible for making the choice which determines the resurrection of which we will be a part.

Except for those who survive the Tribulation, every saint from Adam onward will enter the Millennium in their bodies, transformed into a glorious state, the same state Jesus was after He rose from the grave. He could be touched and felt, but could also walk through walls (John 20:19–29). He was in His glorified state. The apostle Paul wrote, "The dead shall be raised incorruptible, and we shall be changed. For this corruptible must put on incorruption, and this mortal must put on immortality." (1 Cor. 15:52–53).

Our present bodies are quite different from those we shall inhabit in our glorified state. Paul wrote, "There are also celestial bodies, and bodies terrestrial: but the glory of the celestial is one, and the glory of the terrestrial is another. There is one glory of the sun, and another glory of the moon, and another glory of the stars: for one star differeth from another star in glory. So also is the resurrection of the dead. It is sown in corruption; it is raised in incorruption: It is sown in dishonour; it is raised in glory: it is sown in weakness; it is raised in power: It is sown a natural body; it is raised a spiritual body. There is a natural body, and there is a spiritual body" (1 Cor. 15:40–44). He adds, "And as we have borne the image of the earthy, we shall also bear the image of the heavenly" (1 Cor. 15:49).

The Lord Jesus was the first to be resurrected and transformed and will be followed by the Church age saints at the Rapture. At that time, the bodies of all believers who died from Pentecost forward to the Rapture will be resurrected and reunited with their spirits in the air. Scripture says, " For if we believe that Jesus died and rose again, even so them also which sleep in Jesus *will God bring with him.* . . . And the dead in Christ shall rise first" (1 Thess. 4:14,16, italics mine). This means their bodies will rise out of the grave to meet their spirits in the air. All believers who are alive and fortunate enough to experience the Rapture will not face physical death, but will rather be instantly changed into this glorified state. "Behold, I shew you a mystery; We shall not all sleep, but we shall all be changed, In a moment, in the twinkling of an eye" (1 Cor. 15:51–52).

Just as "every one of us shall give account of himself to God" (Rom. 14:12), the Church age saints will be the first group to face judgment at the Judgment Seat of Christ while the Tribulation is taking place on earth. There, believers will be judged for faithful service while on earth and rewarded accordingly (Rom. 14:10; 1 Cor. 3:11–15; 2 Cor. 5:10).

So after Jesus returns to earth at the Second Advent, but before "the saints go marching in" to His millennial kingdom, yet two more groups of believers will be resurrected and judged. Scripture says that then comes "the time of the dead, that they should be judged, and that thou shouldest give reward unto thy servants the prophets, and to the saints, and them that fear thy name, small and great" (Rev. 11:18).

Remember, *everyone* will bow before Christ, and *everyone* will confess Jesus as Lord to the glory of God (Phil. 2:10–11).

The Old Testament Saints. When the Rapture happens, the Old Testament saints will not be included with the Church age saints. Scripture says, "For the Lord himself shall descend from heaven with a shout . . . and the dead *in Christ* shall rise first: Then we which are alive and remain shall be caught up together with them in the clouds, to meet the Lord in the air" (1 Thess. 4:16–17, italics mine). Of course, the Old Testament saints preceded Christ's incarnation, so they are not Raptured with the Church.

They are, in fact, resurrected and judged at the end of the Tribulation after Jesus returns to earth. The prophet Daniel was told that after the "time of trouble, such as never was since there was a nation even to that same time," many of his people "that sleep in the dust of the earth shall awake." He is then told to "go thou thy way till the end be: for thou shalt rest, and stand in thy lot at the end of the days" (Dan. 12:1–2,13).

The prophet Ezekiel was given a vision of a valley full of very dry bones. God tells the bones, "Behold, I will cause breath to enter into you, and ye shall live: And I will lay sinews upon you, and will bring up flesh upon you, and cover you with skin, and put breath in you, and ye shall live" (Ezek. 37:5–6). He then tells Ezekiel the meaning of the vision. "These bones are the whole house of Israel. . . . Behold, O my people, I will open your graves, and cause you to come up out of your graves, and bring you into the land of Israel. . . . And shall put my spirit in you, and ye shall live" (Ezek. 37:11–12,14).

Only believing Israel will be resurrected at that time to enter the Millennium. There will be many who will awake to "shame and everlasting contempt" (Dan. 12:2) at the Great White Throne Judgment.

The Tribulation Saints. Finally, the bodies of the "great multitude, which no man could number, of all nations, and kindreds, and people, and tongues . . . which came out of great tribulation" (Rev. 7:9,14), must also be resurrected and judged before their entry into the Millennium. This takes place at the Second Advent as well. "And I saw the souls of them that were beheaded for the witness of Jesus, and for the word of God . . . and they lived and reigned with Christ a thousand years" (Rev. 20:4).

So the program at Christ's Second Advent provides for all the remaining righteous from the beginning of creation to be resurrected, judged, and transformed into their glorified states before entry into the Millennium. After this, one final resurrection of the dead will take place. The only group remaining are the unsaved dead, or the wicked dead from the beginning of Creation. Their bodies will continue to stay in the grave until after the Millennium, when they will be resurrected to stand before God at the Great White Throne Judgment (Rev. 20:11–15).

At the conclusion of the Tribulation, every saint will have faced judgment except for those who survive the Tribulation, and now they must face judgment and their salvation be determined before entry into the Millennium because, again, no one enters unsaved. These are the ones who will repopulate the earth.

The Judgment Program. Scripture says, "When the Son of man shall come in his glory, and all the holy angels with him, then shall he sit upon the throne of his glory: And before him shall be gathered all nations" (Matt. 25:31–32). It further states, "Whose fan is in his hand, and he will throughly purge his floor, and gather his wheat into the garner; but he will burn up the chaff with unquenchable fire" (Matt. 3:12).

Judgment of Israel. As the nations go, Israel will be first in the order of judgment. At the Second Advent when Jesus returns to earth, He will gather all the Jews scattered from around the world and bring them supernaturally into Israel. Scripture says, "And he shall send his angels with a great sound of a trumpet, and they shall gather together his elect from the four winds, from one end of heaven to the other" (Matt. 24:31). The Lord will bring the Jews into Israel to determine who are saved and who are not.

Once this has been determined, those who believed on the Lord Jesus will enter the Millennium; those who did not will be killed. The prophet Ezekiel wrote,

> And I will bring you out from the people, and will gather you out of the countries wherein ye are scattered, with a mighty hand, and with a stretched out arm, and with fury poured out. And I will bring you into the wilderness of the people, and there will I plead with you face to face. Like as I pleaded with your fathers in the wilderness of the land of Egypt, so will I plead with you, saith the Lord GOD. And I will cause you to pass under the rod, **and** I will bring you into the bond of the covenant: And I **will** purge out from among you the rebels, and them that transgress against me: I will bring them forth out of the country where they sojourn, and they shall not enter into the land of Israel: and ye shall know that I am the LORD.
>
> —Ezekiel 20:34–38

Israel's judgment is depicted in the parable of the ten virgins (Matt. 25:1–13). In this parable, there are five virgins who are prepared and awaiting the arrival of their bridegroom and five who are not. When the announcement is made that the bridegroom is approaching, the five who are unprepared miss his appearance, while the five prepared virgins go into the wedding feast with him. The wedding feast is symbolic of the Millennium.

Israel's judgment is again depicted in the parable of the talents (Matt. 25:14–30). This parable concerns the rewards which are meted out to those who are faithful. In this parable, a man about to go on a journey entrusts his possessions to three of his servants, expecting them to multiply that which he gives them, each according to his own ability. One is given five talents, or units of money, one is given two talents, and one is given one talent. When the man returns from his journey, two of the servants are rewarded for doubling their master's money, while the servant who received one talent does nothing and hides it in the ground. He is symbolic of a man who had the possibility of salvation but chose wickedness instead. He is therefore cast into the outer darkness where there is weeping and gnashing of teeth.

This time of Israel's judgment is what the apostle Paul referred to when he said, "all Israel shall be saved" (Rom. 11:26). He adds, "There shall come out of Sion the Deliverer, and shall turn away ungodliness from Jacob" (Rom. 11:26). The Jews will be brought into Israel to pass under the rod of judgment. Those who rebel and transgress against the Lord will be purged from those who believe, and thereby, all of Israel who enter the Millennium will indeed be saved.

Judgment of Gentile Nations. The twentieth century has already witnessed the offals of evil incarnate. During World War II, Adolf Hitler and his Third Reich slaughtered six million Jews and countless others who did not fit his Aryan agenda. But there were brave German citizens who risked their own lives to help those fleeing Hitler's persecution. The Antichrist's massacre of the Jews will be worldwide, and like so many German citizens, there will be those in all the nations who will attempt to shelter and protect the fleeing Jews. Though this judgment will encompass the nations, salvation will be determined on an individual basis. Again their works do not save them, but rather, distinguish the saved from the unsaved.

The Judgment of Gentile Nations is depicted in the sheep and goat judgment (Matt. 25:31–46). In this passage, the sheep represent the saved, while the goats represent the unsaved. The Lord places the sheep on His right and the goats on His left. He tells the sheep to enter His millennial kingdom because they fed Him, gave Him something to drink, invited Him in as a stranger, clothed Him, visited Him when He was sick and when He was in prison. But they do not understand and question when they did all of this for Him. The Lord responds by saying, "Verily I say unto you, Inasmuch as ye have done it unto one of the least of these my brethren, ye have done it unto me" (Matt. 25:40). He then commands the goats on His left to depart from Him into eternal punishment because when His brothers came to them in the same manner, the goats did nothing to help.

Scripture says,

> Seeing it is a righteous thing with God to recompense tribulation to them that trouble you, And to you who are troubled rest with us, when the Lord Jesus shall be revealed from heaven with his mighty angels, In flaming fire taking vengeance on them that know not God, and that obey not the gospel of our Lord Jesus Christ: Who shall be punished with everlasting destruction from the presence of the Lord, and from the glory of his power; When he shall come to be glorified in his saints, and to be admired in all them that believe (because our testimony among you was believed) in that day.
>
> —2 Thessalonians 1:6–10

Once the Tribulation is finally over, sin and rebellion will be purged from the earth. All the righteous will have been resurrected and judged, the survivors will have faced their judgment, and the Lord Jesus will begin His righteous reign on earth for a thousand years.

Now unto the King eternal, immortal, invisible, the only wise God, be honour and glory for ever and ever. Amen.

—1 Timothy 1:17

Endnotes

1. As quoted by William R. Goetz, *Apocalypse Next* (Horizon Books, Camp Hill, Pennsylvania, 1996), pp. 214–215.
2. J. Dwight Pentecost, *Things to Come* (Zondervan Publishing House, Grand Rapids, Michigan, 1958), p. 340.
3. Ibid., pp. 326–327.
4. Ibid., p. 330.
5. As quoted by William R. Goetz, *Apocalypse Next*, p. 214.
6. Jack Van Impe, *2001: On the Edge of Eternity* (Word Publishing, Dallas, Texas, 1996), p. 76.
7. Ibid., p. 124.
8. As quoted by William R. Goetz, *Apocalypse Next*, p. 206.

And there was given him dominion, and glory, and a king-
dom, that all people, nations, and languages, should serve
him: his dominion is an everlasting dominion, which shall
not pass away, and his kingdom that which shall not be
destroyed.

—Daniel 7:14

Chapter 8

The Millennium

THOUGH WE JUST BEGAN the third millennium, all references in this writing to the Millennium have been to Christ's thousand-year reign on earth. Even if the Church were Raptured today, the seven-year Tribulation must follow before the return of Christ to earth, and therefore, **the recent turn of the millennium should not be confused with the commencement of Christ's Millennial reign.** Indeed, the two millennial references have no connection and are not used interchangeably.

As previously stated, the Millennium will be primarily instituted for the fulfillment of God's covenants made with the nation of Israel. They are the Abrahamic covenant, the Palestinic covenant, and the Davidic covenant. The Millennium will also be established to demonstrate the fallen nature of humanity. With Satan bound in the abyss for a thousand years and the demonic world subdued with him, the source of external temptation will be removed. Yet the wickedness within man's heart will prevail, as we shall see, at the conclusion of the Millennium.

A Theocratic Kingdom

A theocracy is a government established under divine guidance. The governing Authority during the Millennium will be the glorious Lord Jesus Himself (Ps. 2:6–9; Ps. 72; Isa. 9:6–7). He will reign over the whole earth (Ps. 47:8; Isa. 24:23; Zech. 14:9), and David will rule with Him over the nation of Israel (Jer. 30:9; 33:15–17; Ezek. 34:23–24; 37:24–25).

Under David, there will also be rulers, including the twelve disciples who will "sit upon twelve thrones, judging the twelve tribes of Israel" (Isa. 32:1; Jer. 30:21; Matt. 19:28). It is important to note Judas is not one of these twelve disciples. In fact, Jesus said of Judas, "Woe unto that man by whom the Son of man is betrayed! it had been good for that man if he had not been born" (Matt. 26:24). After Judas hung himself for his betrayal of Jesus, the disciples cast lots for who was to fill the vacancy, and it fell to Matthias, who was then counted with the eleven (see Acts 1:16–26).

There will be other subordinate levels of authority as well, all of whom answer to the Lord. Jesus used a parable to describe those who are faithful ruling over cities as a reward for their faithfulness (see Luke 19:11–27). And all who are martyred during the Tribulation will also reign with Him on thrones (Rev. 20:4,6).

In this kingdom, the government will not tolerate sin. With the indwelling Spirit, the knowledge and presence of the Lord, and the removal of external temptation, there is no excuse for sin, and it will therefore be punishable by death (Ps. 2:9; Isa. 29:20–21). "Every one shall die for his own iniquity" (Jer. 31:30).

"The LORD reigneth . . . he shall judge the people righteously" (Ps. 96:10). The Lord's rule will be righteous and just (Isa. 2:3–4; 11:2–5; 32:1). In His kingdom, Jesus is seen as King and Priest. Therefore, Church and state will be one (Ps. 110:1–7; Isa. 66:23; Ezek. 37:26–28; Zech. 14:16–19).

Israel in the Kingdom

At the end of the Tribulation, all of the surviving Jews scattered throughout the world will be supernaturally gathered and brought into Israel (Isa. 27:12; 43:5–7; Jer. 12:15; 24:6; Ezek. 28:25–26; Mic. 4:6; Zeph. 3:20; Matt. 24:31). At that time, their salvation will be determined before entry into the Millennium. The Jews will be restored to their land where they will receive the blessings of the covenants God promised their forefathers.

God promised Abraham that in him, all the families of the earth would be blessed, that his descendants would be given Canaan as an everlasting possession, that his descendants would multiply like the dust of the earth, and that they would all worship God (Gen. 12:1–3; 12:6–7; 13:14–17; 15:1–21; 17:1–14; 22:15–18).

Through the Palestinic covenant, God promised that Israel would fully repent, that all would be converted, and that the Lord would return and restore them to their land (Deut. 30:1–10). It appears Israel's conversion will be a sovereign act of God in keeping with His promise. This covenant served as an extension to the Abrahamic covenant in that it also provided the basis upon which the land of Canaan would someday be occupied by Abraham's descendants.

Finally, God promised David that a child (Solomon) would be born to him who would establish his kingdom and build the Temple, and that David's house, throne, and kingdom would last forever (2 Sam. 7:12–16).

During the Millennium, all these covenants with Israel will be fulfilled. The nation was joined to God by marriage (Ezek. 16:8–14), and at this time, their relationship to Him as their Husband will be renewed (Isa. 54:5–7; 62:2–5; Hos. 2:19–20). As the chosen of God, Israel will also be exalted over the Gentiles (Isa. 14:1–2; 49:22–23). "The sons also of them that afflicted thee shall come bending unto thee; and all they that despised thee shall bow themselves down at the soles of thy feet; and they shall call thee, The city of the LORD, The Zion of the Holy One of Israel" (Isa. 60:14).

Because of the ruin of Palestine during the latter half of the Tribulation, Israel will be reconstructed during this time (Isa. 61:4; Ezek. 36:33–38; Amos 9:14), and its borders extended to include all the land promised to Abraham (Gen. 15:18–21; Isa. 26:15; Obad. 19–20). The twelve tribes of Israel will each receive their apportioned land, including the tribe of Dan (Ezek. 48:1–29). And the "holy oblation," a squared territory consisting of thirty-four square miles in each direction, will be set apart for the Lord (Ezek. 48:8–20).

Gentiles in the Kingdom

All the surviving Gentiles at the conclusion of the Tribulation will face judgment to determine their salvation before entry into the Millennium. Those who are saved will enter and inherit the universal blessings of the Abrahamic covenant. The apostle Paul wrote, "And if ye be Christ's, then are ye Abraham's seed, and heirs according to the promise" (Gal. 3:29). All will be under the Lordship of Jesus as King, and for a thousand years, the Gentiles will be second to the Jews, who are given favor by God during this period (Isa. 14:1–2; 49:22–23; 60:14).

Spiritual Life in the Kingdom

The born-again who survive the Tribulation will enter the Millennium in their physical bodies to repopulate the earth (Isa. 26:2; 60:21; Matt. 25:37). Of course, children who have not reached the age of accountability will also enter, but personal faith in Christ will be required of them and their descendants, who will be born with a sin nature. Once they receive Christ, the Holy Spirit will indwell them as believers. There are a number of Scripture references which relate to the indwelling Spirit during the Millennium (Isa. 32:15; 44:3; 59:21; Ezek. 36:26–27; 37:14; 39:29; Joel 2:28–29). During this period, spiritual life will be different than at any other time since Creation. There will be universal spiritual truth, the knowledge of God throughout the world (Jer. 31:34). Jesus will dwell among man (Zech. 2:10–13; Rev. 21:3), and the whole earth will be filled with the glory of God (Ps. 72:19). Satan will be bound and the demonic world will be restrained, so there will be nothing evil to influence man's heart. The earth will be full of righteousness. "The Lord GOD will cause righteousness and praise to spring forth before all the nations" (Isa. 61:11). It will be a time of willing obedience to the Lord, a time of joy inexpressible, a time of heartfelt passion for the Lord.

Unlike the numerous religions which exist today, there will be one faith. All the world will be united in worshiping the Lord God (Isa. 45:23; 52:10; 66:20–23; Zeph. 3:9; Zech. 14:16; Mal. 1:11).

The Millennial Temple

Ezekiel went into great detail in describing the millennial Temple. He also described the throne, the altar, priestly service, and worship rituals (Ezek. 40:1–46:24). The Lord Jesus will reign over the world from this Temple (Ezek. 43:7), built on the thirty-four–square–mile site of the "holy oblation." It will be eight hundred seventy-five feet in length and width, towering three stories high, with thirty rooms on each level (Ezek. 41:5–7). It will face in an easterly direction and be completely surrounded by a wall, with gates on all sides but the west. Just on the inside of the wall will be the outer courtyard, where the people will assemble. There will also be an elevated inner courtyard, accessible by three gates, all of which are opposite the gates in the outer wall. The Lord declared this "the place of my throne, and the place of the soles of my feet, where I will dwell in the midst of the children of Israel for ever" (Ezek. 43:7).

During the Millennium, worship rituals will resume to include animal sacrifices through burnt offerings, sin offerings, and guilt offerings (Isa. 56:7; Jer. 33:18; Ezek. 40:39; 46:13). This sacrificial system will not be established for the atonement of sin, but as a memorial to the accomplished work of redemption.

Everday Life in the Kingdom

It appears the organizational structure and routine of life will continue in the Millennium much as it does today, except man will live in a near-perfect environment under a righteous King and Priest. As such, the established order of things will be fully under His control, and sin will not be tolerated. For a thousand years, our Lord will showcase to the world and to the universe what life could have been like all this time in the beautiful state which God intended. There are a number of Scripture references which characterize what everyday life will be like in the millennial kingdom. Here are just a few.

There will finally be lasting peace on earth. "And the work of righteousness shall be peace; and the effect of righteousness quietness and assurance for ever" (Isa. 32:17).

There will be night and day, but the light of both will be brilliant. "Moreover the light of the moon shall be as the light of the sun, and the light of the sun shall be sevenfold, as the light of seven days" (Isa. 30:26).

There will be no more sickness. "And the inhabitant shall not say, I am sick" (Isa. 33:24). "For I will restore health unto thee, and I will heal thee of thy wounds, saith the LORD" (Jer. 30:17). Before entry into the Millennium, He will correct any deformities. "And in that day shall the deaf hear the words of the book, and the eyes of the blind shall see" (Isa. 29:18).

Society will be industrialized. "And they shall build houses, and inhabit them; and they shall plant vineyards, and eat the fruit of them" (Isa. 65:21).

There will be economic prosperity for everyone. "Therefore they shall come and sing in the height of Zion, and shall flow together to the goodness of the LORD, for wheat, and for wine, and for oil, and for the young of the flock and of the herd: and their soul shall be as a watered garden; and they shall not sorrow any more at all. Then shall the virgin rejoice in the dance, both young men and old together: for I will turn their mourning into joy, and will comfort them, and make them rejoice from their sorrow" (Jer. 31:12–13).

Just as before the Flood, *lifespans will be lengthened.* "There shall be no more thence an infant of days, nor an old man that hath not filled his days: for the child shall die an hundred years old; but the sinner being an hundred years old shall be accursed" (Isa. 65:20).

Lastly, *the animal kingdom will be changed.* "The wolf also shall dwell with the lamb, and the leopard shall lie down with the kid; and the calf and the young lion and the fatling together; and a little child shall lead them. And the cow and the bear shall feed; their young ones shall lie down together: and the lion shall eat straw like the ox. And the sucking child shall play on the hole of the asp, and the weaned child shall put his hand on the cockatrice' den. They shall not hurt nor destroy in all my holy mountain: for the earth shall be full of the knowledge of the LORD, as the waters cover the sea" (Isa. 11:6–9).

The Heavenly Jerusalem

Scripture says, "But ye are come unto mount Sion, and unto the city of the living God, the heavenly Jerusalem, and to an innumerable company of angels, To the general assembly and church of the firstborn, which are written in heaven, and to God the Judge of all, and to the spirits of just men made perfect, And to Jesus the mediator of the new covenant" (Heb. 12:22–24).

We have seen at the conclusion of the Tribulation that there will be a program of resurrection and judgment. At that time the bodies of all the righteous before the Day of Pentecost as well as those of the Tribulation martyrs will be resurrected and reunited with their spirits to face judgment and receive their eternal rewards. We saw that the Church age saints will have experienced this seven years earlier at the Rapture, where they will then stand in heaven before the Judgment Seat of Christ to receive their eternal rewards.

All of these saints will have been translated into their glorified bodies, and together with the holy angels, this mighty assembly will enter the Millennium where they will live in the heavenly Jerusalem. It appears that at the Second Advent when the Lord Jesus returns to earth, the heavenly Jerusalem will descend (Rev. 21:10) and hover over the earth where Jerusalem is today.

The living saints who will have survived the Tribulation will enter the Millennium in their natural bodies, where they will continue to live on the earth and repopulate it. They will not be able to enter the heavenly Jerusalem, for only those living in glorified states can enter. But this is not so for the translated saints, who can freely come and go from the heavenly Jerusalem to earth. Just as Jesus walked among men in His glorified state after His resurrection, so will the translated saints walk among the living saints on the earth during the Millennium.

As part of the governing body in the Lord's theocratic kingdom, the translated saints will sit on thrones in various capacities and judge the world. The apostle Paul wrote, "Do ye not know that the saints shall judge the world?" (1 Cor. 6:2). During the Millennium, only those living on the earth will be subject to the Lord's reign, not those living in the heavenly Jerusalem. These translated saints will have already been brought under His authority, and as such, will be part of His administration of righteousness.

As Jesus approached Jerusalem nearly two thousand years ago, He gave the parable of a nobleman who was going away to a distant country to receive a kingdom (Luke 19:11–27). Once he received it, he would return. So he called his servants and gave them each a sum of money to conduct business while he was away. When he returned, he summoned them to see what business they had done. One earned ten times the amount he was given, to which the nobleman replied, "Well done," adding, "because you have been faithful in a very little thing, be in authority over ten cities." Each who increased his money was granted authority over cities equal in number to what he had earned. This parable was used to show the rewards for servitude, and likewise applies to the faithful saints who will be given authority over many cities when the King returns.

At the end of the Millennium, it appears the heavenly Jerusalem and all its occupants will ascend back into heaven as God destroys the earth for the final time.

Thy kingdom come. Thy will be done in earth, as it is in heaven.

—**Matthew 6:10**

Chapter 9

After the Millennium, Then What?

The Second War of Gog and Magog

THOUGH MAN WILL LIVE in a near-perfect environment for a thousand years, in the presence of the Lord Jesus and with the full knowledge of God, there will be a final uprising which will attest to the sinful, wicked nature of the human heart, a heart which can only be changed by the grace of God when we receive a new nature through salvation. This war is the final conflict for mankind. It will occur at the conclusion of the thousand-year reign of Christ, and the participants will be "as the sand of the sea" (Rev. 20:8).

Before the Millennium begins, Satan will be bound in chains and thrown into the abyss where he will stay for a thousand years (Rev. 20:1–3). But "when the thousand years are expired, Satan shall be loosed out of his prison, And shall go out to deceive the nations which are in the four quarters of the earth, Gog and Magog, to gather them together to battle" (Rev. 20:7–8).

This war is not to be confused with the one occurring around the midpoint of the Tribulation, as recorded in Ezekiel 38 and 39. There is uncertainty as to why two wars of the same name occur, but clearly a number of differences exist between the two. Ezekiel describes a coalition of only a few nations invading Israel; whereas in the second war, all the nations are gathered against Jerusalem. Ezekiel records Gog's alliance on the northern mountains of Israel; whereas in this second war, the participants are on the broad plain surrounding Jerusalem. Ezekiel makes no mention of Satan's direct intervention; whereas in the second war, he is the catalyst for the uprising. Ezekiel records Gog's destruction by forces of nature combined with man-made weapons of destruction, and afterward, a period of seven months to bury the dead and seven years to dispose of the debris. In this second war, the invaders are consumed by fire which "came down from God out of heaven, and devoured them" (Rev. 20:9), leaving no bodies to be buried. Ezekiel records the millennial kingdom to follow; whereas after the second war, no life continues, but rather, the heavens and the earth are totally destroyed.

Scripture does not indicate how long the war will last, only that after Satan has been bound for a thousand years, "he must be loosed a little season" (Rev. 20:3).

Judgment on Satan and the Fallen Angels

After Satan's release and final attempt to overthrow God, he will be cast into the eternal lake of fire (Rev. 20:10), as his earthly kingdom finally comes to an end. He will then no longer be the prince and power of the air. The Antichrist and False Prophet will have already been in the lake of fire a thousand years when Satan joins them. There, they will be "tormented day and night for ever and ever" (Rev. 20:10).

But judgment still awaits the angels who followed Satan in his rebellion against God. Scripture says, "And the angels which kept not their first estate, but left their own habitation, he hath reserved in everlasting chains under darkness unto the judgment of the great day" (Jude 6). The apostle Peter wrote, "God spared not the angels that sinned, but cast them down to hell, and delivered them into chains of darkness, to be reserved unto judgment" (2 Pet. 2:4). When Satan is cast into the lake of fire, his minions will be thrown in there with him. Their judgment is one I surely hope to see.

The New Heavens and the New Earth

The satanically led revolt against God at the conclusion of the Millennium will bring the armies of the world again to Jerusalem where God will consume them by fire. At that point, He will also destroy the world by fire. The apostle Peter wrote, "But the heavens and the earth, which are now, by the same word are kept in store, reserved unto fire against the day of judgment and perdition of ungodly men. . . . But the day of the Lord will come as a thief in the night; in the which the heavens shall pass away with a great noise, and the elements shall melt with fervent heat, the earth also and the works that are therein shall be burned up" (2 Pet. 3:7,10).

Because Adam and Eve sinned in the Garden of Eden, a curse was placed on the earth by God (Gen. 3:17; 5:29). Scripture says, "For the creature was made subject to vanity, not willingly, but by reason of him who hath subjected the same in hope, Because the creature itself also shall be delivered from the bondage of corruption into the glorious liberty of the children of God. For we know that the whole creation groaneth and travaileth in pain together until now" (Rom. 8:20–22).

Simply put, sin defiles everything, and by God's very nature, He cannot be in the presence of sin. So before God Himself makes His dwelling among men (Rev. 21:3), the earth must be destroyed and reformed in purity. Our infinite God will create another earth for Himself and His family.

John the apostle wrote, "And I saw a new heaven and a new earth: for the first heaven and the first earth were passed away" (Rev. 21:1). And God said, "Behold, I make all things new" (Rev. 21:5).

The Great White Throne Judgment

Once the earth is purged, the unsaved dead will stand before God at the Great White Throne Judgment. "And I saw a great white throne, and him that sat on it, from whose face the earth and the heaven fled away; and there was found no place for them" (Rev. 20:11). This is the final resurrection and judgment. Remember, before entry into Christ's millennial kingdom, every righteous person from the beginning of Creation will face their day of judgment. At that point, the only ones who remain to be judged are the unsaved dead, those who did not choose life through Jesus Christ or put their faith in God before Pentecost.

How many of us have heard someone say, "If I'm going to hell, at least my friends will be there"? It grieves me to know there will be good people there who did not see the importance of choosing Jesus Christ while they were alive. They did not understand or accept the reality of the atonement of sin through His blood, and they died forever separated from Him. Hell is a place of consciousness, and they will remember all the times someone told them of Jesus and what He did for them on the Cross. The only reason God entered this world in the form of a man was "to seek and to save that which was lost" (Luke 19:10). That was you, that was me, that was all of us before we responded to His love. He calls everyone, but He has given us a free will to decide for ourselves whether we will respond and invite Him into our hearts. He says, "Behold, I stand at the door, and knock: if any man hear my voice, and open the door, I will come in to him, and will sup with him, and he with me" (Rev. 3:20).

So many people get hung up on, "I can't believe a loving God will send all these billions of people to hell because they don't believe as Christians do." The fact of the matter is, He is not sending anyone to hell. We send ourselves to hell. *Everyone* has the opportunity to come to Him—*everyone*. Scripture says, "God is no respecter of persons: But in every nation he that feareth him, and worketh righteousness, is accepted with him" (Acts 10:34–35). And, "*whosoever* shall call upon the name of the Lord shall be saved" (Rom. 10:13, italics mine).

We cannot live any way we want. There are eternal consequences to our actions, and if you choose to live your short life on this earth and not respond to His love, then do not be fooled into believing when you die, you will spend eternity with a holy God. Contrary to what the world tells you, life is not about the pursuit of happiness, but the pursuit of pleasing God. We were created for His good pleasure (Rev. 4:11), and we should "labour, that . . . we may be accepted of him" (2 Cor. 5:9). A right-standing relationship with the Lord then creates a heart overflowing with joy, even in the midst of difficult circumstances.

Indeed, there will be more people in hell than in heaven. Jesus said, "Enter ye in at the strait gate: for wide is the gate, and broad is the way, that leadeth to destruction, and many there be which go in thereat: Because strait is the gate, and narrow is the way, which leadeth unto life, and few there be that find it" (Matt. 7:13–14).

When the unsaved die, their bodies go to the grave, while their spirits descend into hell, a place of torment. However, hell is not the final resting place for the wicked dead. At the Great White Throne Judgment, the bodies of the unsaved are resurrected and reunited with their spirits to stand before God. For a brief moment, they will have a reprieve from their torment to stand in His all-consuming, holy presence where they too will bow their knees and confess Jesus as Lord (Phil. 2:10–11). Once they are judged, they will be cast into the lake of fire, where they will stay forever. Scripture says, "And I saw a great white throne, and him that sat on it . . . And I saw the dead, small and great, stand before God; and the books were opened: and another book was opened, which is the book of life: and the dead were judged out of those things which were written in the books, according to their works. . . . And whosoever was not found written in the book of life was cast into the lake of fire" (Rev. 20:11–12,15).

When we choose Jesus Christ as our personal Savior, He comes to take up residence in our hearts through the Holy Spirit (John 14:16–17; Rom. 8:11; Eph. 3:16–17). At that very moment, our names are recorded in the Book of Life forever. As human beings, we are so limited by time that we cannot conceive of time never ending, but be assured, each one of us will live eternally either with God or separated from Him, and when a billion years has passed, then there will be another billion, and another, and another.

Dear reader, *please listen*. Someday, *you are going to die*, but you do not know when your soul will be required of you. So "to day if ye will hear his voice, Harden not your heart" (Ps. 95:7–8). IF you have not already done so, then right now, get on your knees and acknowledge Jesus as Lord, that you realize He came to pay the price for sin, and that you are a sinner in need of forgiveness. Ask Him to forgive you of your sins and invite Him to come into your heart.

If you are sincere, He will take up residence within you through the Holy Spirit (John 14:16–17; 2 Tim. 1:14), and you will slowly begin to change into conformity to His likeness. Scripture says, "That if thou shalt confess with thy mouth the Lord Jesus, and shalt believe in thine heart that God hath raised him from the dead, thou shalt be saved. For with the heart man believeth unto righteousness; and with the mouth confession is made unto salvation" (Rom. 10:9–10). You will experience life abundantly, and most assuredly, you will be spared the Great White Throne Judgment.

The New Jerusalem
With a newly created heaven and earth, the eternal city of the

New Jerusalem will descend to earth. It is not possible to describe our eternal abode and do it justice, but one thing is sure, "Eye hath not seen, nor ear heard, neither have entered into the heart of man, the things which God hath prepared for them that love him" (1 Cor. 2:9).

Close your eyes for a moment and picture the most pristine thing you have ever seen. Perhaps it is a place high in the mountains, a place you have found where not a hint of civilization has been. Or maybe it was a sunset so brilliant you stopped what you were doing to gaze at what looked like fire in the sky. Now try to recall a sound you have heard that was so soothing to your ears that it made you smile and close your eyes to fully appreciate. Perhaps it was the magnificence of nature, or a symphony, or maybe a child calling home just to tell you of their love. Whatever it is, the most wonderful thing your eyes and ears have experienced will not compare to what our loving Father has in store. Just as we want the best for our children, our infinite Creator God wants the very best for us, and while we are limited in what we can give our children, He is not. So we are assured by the apostle Paul, who was caught up to the third heaven (2 Cor. 12:1–4), "that which has not entered the heart of man" awaits.

While we cannot fully comprehend what God has prepared for us, we do have a brief description of our eternal dwelling. The new earth will be a gigantic land mass, having not sea at all (Rev. 21:1). During the Millennium, the heavenly Jerusalem will be *over* the earth in the place where Jerusalem is today. It will be a literal, eternal city, having the squared dimensions of a cube, fifteen hundred miles in length, width, and height (Rev. 21:16). Look at a map of the United States. The city's dimensions will cover an area from Seattle to Minneapolis, down to Houston, and over to Los Angeles, though the distance from Los Angeles to Seattle falls short some four hundred miles. That is an enormous city, and it goes up into the sky fifteen hundred miles as well. No doubt it is that of which Jesus spoke when He said, "In my Father's house are many mansions. . . . I go to prepare a place for you" (John 14:2).

The wall surrounding the New Jerusalem is equally staggering to the imagination. It will be two hundred sixteen feet high and made of jasper, a green-colored stone which is described as "clear as crystal" (Rev. 21:11,17,18). It will have twelve foundations made of precious stones, each foundation bearing the name of one of the twelve apostles (Rev. 21:14,19,20). The wall will have twelve gates, three in each direction of the compass (Rev. 21:12–13). Each gate will be made of a single pearl, each bearing the name of one of the twelve tribes of Israel (Rev. 21:12,21), and angels will be stationed at all twelve of the gates (Rev. 21:12).

There will be no Temple in the New Jerusalem, "for the Lord God Almighty and the Lamb are the temple of it" (Rev. 21:22). There will be "no need of the sun, neither of the moon, to shine in it: for the glory of God did lighten it, and the Lamb is the light thereof" (Rev. 21:23).

The street of the eternal city will be pure gold, "as it were transparent glass" (Rev. 21:21). And on either side of the river will be the tree of life, bearing twelve kinds of fruit every month (Rev. 22:2).

At that point and forever more, God will dwell among men, and "we shall see him as he is" (1 John 3:2). There will be no more tears, no more death, no more mourning, no more crying, and no more pain (Rev. 21:4). And for that, I joyfully shout hallelujah and praise to our glorious Lord God on high! Yes, "I will praise thy name for ever and ever" (Ps. 145:2).

I am the way, the truth, and the life: no man cometh unto the Father, but by me.

—**John 14:6**

Chapter 10

One Way Out ... One Way In

P LEASE PAY CLOSE ATTENTION. Jesus is on the verge of receiving unto Himself His bride, the Church. When He does, all who are left behind will suffer the horrors of the Tribulation. For those who would like to avoid this hellish nightmare, there is only one way out. For those who want to behold God and dwell with Him in His glorious eternal kingdom, there is only one way in. Both ways are the same, and that is through the Lord Jesus Christ. Jesus said, "I am the way, the truth, and the life: no man cometh unto the Father, but by me." (John 14:6).

In its simplest form, here is the story of man's separation from God. When God created Adam and Eve, He set them in a perfect environment in the Garden of Eden. He told them they could eat freely of any tree in the garden, except the tree of the knowledge of good and evil, that if they ate of this tree, they would surely die. Satan, the liar and destroyer, tempted Eve, offering her fruit from the very tree of which God told them they could not eat. He twisted God's words, as he always does, and Eve took of the fruit, ate it, and encouraged Adam to do so as well (see Gen. 2–3).

This act was in direct disobedience to what God had instructed, and it was the first sin ever committed by man. God walked and talked with Adam and Eve in a perfect, sinless environment, but when they disobeyed Him, they fell from God and sin wedged between God and man. God is absolute holiness, and He cannot be in the presence of sin, not because He would rather not be, but because He cannot be. Adam and Eve became the embodiment of sin for all of mankind. Scripture says, "For none of us liveth to himself" (Rom. 14:7). So as a result of their actions, every human being born thereafter is born into a sin nature, and "the wages of sin is death" (Rom. 6:23). Scripture says, "Wherefore, as by one man sin entered into the world, and death by sin; and so death passed upon all men, for that all have sinned" (Rom. 5:12).

After Adam and Eve sinned, they were cast out of the garden to prevent them from continuing to eat of the tree of life. Had they done so, they would have lived forever in their sinful condition, and there would have been no means of reconciliation to God. Even though God knew we would sin, He created us with a free will; the ability to make our own decisions. He could have stopped them, but He allowed it because by His very nature, He will not coerce our will. But even before the sin was ever committed, God had a plan for our redemption.

Scripture says, "And almost all things are by the law purged with blood; and without shedding of blood is no remission" (Heb. 9:22). So for thousands of years while the Messianic lineage was borne out, our guilt was symbolically transferred to an innocent substitute through faith. Every year, the high priest would enter the Temple and sacrifice a perfect, unblemished lamb as an acceptable offering to God for the sins of the people.

Then came the time for the birth of Jesus, the Savior of the world. Because of God's incomprehensible love for mankind, Jesus left His adored Father in heaven and came into the world through a virgin (Matt. 1:18–25; Luke 1:26–38) specifically and only to pay the price for man's sin once and for all (Heb. 7:27; 10:10). It was the greatest act of love mankind would ever know.

Animal sacrifices were no longer an acceptable atonement to God for sin. But in fact, "he hath made him to be sin for us, who knew no sin; that we might be made the righteousness of God in him" (2 Cor. 5:21). The Father placed man's sin on Jesus as the perfect, unblemished Lamb of God, and He willingly went to the Cross and died (1 Pet. 1:18–19; 2:24). His death paid the price for mankind's sin forevermore. "This is a faithful saying, and worthy of all acceptation, that Christ Jesus came into the world to save sinners" (1 Tim. 1:15). And now man is reconciled to God through Him.

Scripture says, "Neither is there salvation in any other: for there is none other name under heaven given among men, whereby we must be saved" (Acts 4:12). If you have not received Jesus Christ, you must stop believing Satan's lies that you are going to heaven when you die because you are not.

Likewise, do not believe Satan's lies that you are going to heaven because you are a good person. You will not. Scripture says, "there is none that doeth good, no, not one," and that "all have sinned, and come short of the glory of God" (Rom. 3:12,23). In fact, on our very best day, God says our righteousness is as filthy rags (Isa. 64:6). Being good will not get you to heaven. I cannot stress that enough. Your eternal destination has absolutely nothing to do with being good.

It is ONLY by faith that we are saved. "Therefore being justified by faith, we have peace with God through our Lord Jesus Christ" (Rom. 5:1). Scripture says, "For by grace are ye saved through faith; and that not of yourselves: it is the gift of God: Not of works, lest any man should boast" (Eph. 2:8–9). "And if by grace, then is it no more of works: otherwise grace is no more grace" (Rom. 11:6). By its very definition, "grace" means unmerited favor. So you cannot work your way into heaven by doing a single thing. Salvation is free, *totally free.* Scripture says, "the gift of God is eternal life through Jesus Christ our Lord" (Rom. 6:23). We cannot *do* anything to receive it except believe in Jesus Christ and what He did for us on the Cross. "Who his own self bare our sins in his own body on the tree, that we, being dead to sins, should live unto righteousness: by whose stripes ye were healed" (1 Pet. 2:24).

Do you want salvation? It is available to anyone who wants it. Jesus said, "Behold, I stand at the door, and knock: if any man hear my voice, and open the door, I will come in to him, and will sup with him, and he with me" (Rev. 3:20). All you have to do is open the door and let Him in, and you must be willing to turn from sin. It is that simple. Satan is the one who has complicated the process and muddied the waters so much with his lies that people find it hard to believe that is all there is to it. I did not say you must not sin again; I said you must be willing to turn from your sin. Believe me, you will still sin from the day you receive the Lord Jesus into your life until the day you stand before Him in glory, but your sins are forgiven.

Remember, bloodshed is the only acceptable atonement for sin. When we accept Jesus as our Lord and Savior, His blood cleanses us from our unrighteousness in the sight of God. Our sins are completely forgiven. Scripture says, "through his name whosoever believeth in him shall receive remission of sins" (Acts 10:43). Those committed in the past, present, and future are remembered no more (Heb. 8:12; 10:17). Our transgressions are removed from us as far as the east is from the west (Ps. 103:12). They are nailed to the Cross (Col. 2:13–14). At that point, all God sees when He looks at you and me is Christ Jesus living on the inside of us.

Really, think about it. Why would God make salvation any more difficult than simply repenting and believing in Jesus?

He loves His creation. God wants us to spend eternity with Him, but that is only possible through His Son. "For God so loved the world, that he gave his only begotten Son, that whosoever believeth in him should not perish, but have everlasting life. For God sent not his Son into the world to condemn the world; but that the world through him might be saved" (John 3:16–17). And, "God our Saviour, Who will have all men to be saved, and to come unto the knowledge of the truth. For there is one God, and one mediator between God and men, the man Christ Jesus" (1 Tim. 2:3–5).

So I ask you again. Do you want eternal life? Do you want a way out of the coming Tribulation? Do you want a way into the eternal kingdom? If you do, then get on your knees right now and pray this prayer out loud and from a sincere heart:

The Sinner's Prayer

Dear Lord Jesus,

I realize I am a sinner whose sins can only be forgiven by the blood You shed for me that day on Calvary. Oh, Lord, I know and believe with all of my heart that You came into this world through a virgin, lived a sinless life, and after You were crucified, God raised You from the dead and seated You at His right hand. Lord, I want You to come into my life and take up residence in my heart. I am willing to turn from sin and place all my trust in You. Jesus, thank You for paying the price for my sin. Thank You that if I were the only one to be lost, You would have still come and died just for me.

In your precious name I pray. Amen.

Scripture says, "That if thou shalt confess with thy mouth the Lord Jesus, and shalt believe in thine heart that God hath raised him from the dead, thou shalt be saved. For with the heart man believeth unto righteousness; and with the mouth confession is made unto salvation" (Rom. 10:9–10). If you prayed that prayer from a sincere heart, Jesus came to take up residence within you. You have been sealed "with that holy Spirit of promise, Which is the earnest of our inheritance until the redemption of the purchased possession, unto the praise of his glory" (Eph. 1:13–14). In other words, you are sealed, until God calls you home to glory (John 14:16–17; 2 Cor. 1:22; Eph. 4:30). You can *never* lose your salvation. And *do not let Satan convince you otherwise*, because he is going to try.

God will begin the work of perfecting you "until the day of Jesus Christ" (Phil. 1:6). It is a very slow process, and you are going to sin and make mistakes, and Satan will tempt you repeatedly. But *he is a liar*. In fact, Jesus called him "a liar, and the father of it" (John 8:44). If he can get you to doubt your salvation, then you will become less of a threat to him in leading others to the Lord by telling them what Jesus has done for you. When you sin, and you will, confess it, repent, and move on. Scripture says, "If we confess our sins, he is faithful and just to forgive us our sins, and to cleanse us from all unrighteousness" (1 John 1:9). Indeed, your sins were forgiven the moment you invited Jesus into your heart, but when we sin, we also need to confess it because sin breaks the fellowship we enjoy with God.

Finally, just as you eat food to keep your body strong, you also need food to keep your Spirit strong. Scripture says, "As newborn babes, desire the sincere milk of the word, that ye may grow thereby" (1 Pet. 2:2). When you do not eat, you gradually weaken physically. So it is with the Spirit. You must discipline yourself to read the Bible daily and pray or else your spiritual state will gradually weaken. The importance of this daily regimen simply cannot be overstated. Find a Bible teaching church where you can plant your roots and grow with the body of Christ. In a forest, you never see one tree toppled over with its roots pulled out of the ground because the roots are all intertwined. In the same way, the body of Christ will help strengthen you against the enemy so you will stand strong in the storms of life.

A Pastor's Prayer

Heavenly Father,

I pray Your hedge of protection around these new baby believers. I ask that You bind the attacks of discouragement and doubt. Lord, will You open their eyes and their hearts so they may know You and the power of Your Word in their lives. Father, send people who will surround them and help them grow spiritually in the knowledge of who You are. Lord God, I ask that You give them a passionate heart to follow You in all of Your glorious ways. And, Father, I pray that You enable them to trust You implicitly.

Lord, I ask all these things in Jesus' name. Amen.

Let me be the first to welcome you to the eternal family as my new brother or sister in Christ. Our Lord Jesus said, "I say unto you, there is joy in the presence of the angels of God over one sinner that repenteth" (Luke 15:10). Just think of it, the Lord and the angels and all the children of God in His presence are rejoicing right now over the decision you just made, and I am delighted as well that we will be spending eternity together with our glorious Lord God. I look forward to seeing you there!

—Dr. John R. Bisagno

About the Author

John R. Bisagno was born in Augusta, Kansas, in 1934. He graduated from Oklahoma Baptist University and received his Doctor of Letters degree from Southwest Missouri Baptist University and his Doctor of Divinity degree from Houston Baptist University, where a "Chair of Evangelism" is named in his honor. Dr. Bisagno has been the pastor of Houston's First Baptist Church for thirty years. Dr. Bisagno has authored twenty-two books and was president of the Southern Baptist Pastor's Conference in 1972.